An instructional aid for worker students

Series:
Trade Union Functions and Services

A Guide to the Teaching of Collective Bargaining

Tore Nyman

International Labour Office   Geneva

ISBN 92-2-102867-4

First published 1981

The designations employed in ILO publications, which are in conformity with United Nations practice, and the presentation of material therein do not imply the expression of any opinion whatsoever on the part of the International Labour Office concerning the legal status of any country or territory or of its authorities, or concerning the delimitation of its frontiers.
The responsibility for opinions expressed in signed articles, studies and other contributions rests solely with their authors, and publication does not constitute an endorsement by the International Labour Office of the opinions expressed in them.

ILO publications can be obtained through major booksellers or ILO local offices in many countries, or direct from ILO Publications, International Labour Office, CH-1211 Geneva 22, Switzerland. A catalogue or list of new publications will be sent free of charge from the above address.

Printed by the International Labour Office, Geneva, Switzerland

Contents

I. INTRODUCTION

In modern society, collective bargaining at different levels is the most important function through which a trade union endeavours to accomplish its tasks - improving working and living conditions for the members. Collective bargaining is at the same time an essential characteristic of a sound industrial relations system, recognised as such by workers, employers and governments alike. It is hardly surprising that it is the concern of a major ILO Convention, the Right to Organise and Collective Bargaining Convention (No. 98) of 1949, as well as an important Recommendation, the Collective Agreements Recommendation (No. 91) of 1951. The former asserts the right; the latter enumerates some of the essential conditions for making the right effective.

The different forms which collective bargaining can take will be touched on later in this guide. One thing they all have in common is that they are examples of representative democracy. They consist in a representative or representatives stating a case for the members of their constituency. The constituency may be the entire labour force of a nation, or even, at the international level (within the ILO, for example) of many nations, the workers of the world. At the other extreme, the constituency may be a single worker who has been unjustly treated, or feels himself to have been so treated, in whose defence the representative speaks with the collective voice of all his fellows, who know that some day they may find themselves in need of the same protection.

Whatever the case, whether he speaks for one man or for a multitude, the burden resting on the representative's shoulders is heavy indeed. It is clearly of the utmost importance, not only to working men and women, but to society as a whole, that the members of trade unions should understand the collective bargaining process, should appreciate its possibilities and its limitations, and that workers' representatives should be competent to discharge their responsibilities in this all-important field. In developing countries in particular, because of their relatively limited experience, there is a growing demand for trade union courses in collective bargaining. That is why the ILO Workers' Education Branch was asked to prepare this guide.

The guide is not about collective bargaining as such. It is about the teaching of collective bargaining, teaching what collective bargaining is and the skills required to participate in it as a workers' representative. The reader wishing to study the collective bargaining process has a wealth of material at his disposal, including the ILO Workers' Education Manual Collective Bargaining. Similarly, the guide is not an introduction to adult education techniques. There, again, the worker wishing to study the subject can turn to a number of other publications, among them the ILO Workers' Education Manual Workers' Education and its Techniques and series of eight booklets prepared by the ILO Workers' Education Branch for the guidance of workers' educators at local and branch level.[1]

----

[1] The Theory of Communication; Simple Reproduction Techniques; The Use of Sound in Workers' Education; Selected Methods for Workers' Education; Lettering and Drawing - Do-it-Yourself; Projection Arrangements and Overhead Projector; The Teacher's

(Footnote continued on next page)

What this guide does is simply make some suggestions about the methods to be used in the teaching of a chosen subject, collective bargaining. The assumption must be that the reader is fairly familiar with the techniques normally available to the adult educator and that he knows what it is he wishes to teach under the heading "collective bargaining". Yet it would clearly be absurd to leave it at that. Before a particular method can be selected for imparting a given piece of knowledge, obviously the piece of knowledge must first be identified and the manner in which the chosen method may be applied must then be explained. Hence this guide, as it goes along, must inevitably analyse the collective bargaining process in some little detail, if only to break it down into convenient modules for teaching purposes.

Or, rather, the guide must help the reader to make that analysis. It cannot be too strongly emphasised that trade union educators themselves must decide what it is they wish to teach, and to whom. Although a very broad definition of collective bargaining can no doubt be agreed, the scope and possibilities of collective bargaining itself differ greatly in different countries, and indeed in different industries and sectors. In no two nations is the process exactly the same. Therefore, each educational unit - be it a national labour federation, an individual trade union or a workplace group - must make its own definitions of collective bargaining in terms of its members' interests and the part they play in the process. No outside body can do that for them. All this guide can do is list some of the possibilities. The practical educator will extract what is useful in his particular case, discard what is irrelevant and add what has been missed out.

The statement made above, that one of our assumptions must be that "the reader knows what it is he wishes to teach", obviously does not mean that he knows what to teach without having given the matter serious thought. The drafting of an appropriate syllabus for the intended study group is possibly the most important task facing those responsible for workers' education. When the weaknesses of trade union courses are dissected, it is nearly always found that one of the main causes of failure or of inadequacy is that the syllabus has been off-target. "Get the content right, and the course will take care of itself" may be not the whole truth, but it is a very important aspect of the truth. Only programme planners themselves, however, and with them the members who are to take part in a given course, can know what it is they wish to teach and to learn. All this guide can do is roughly outline a model framework which, it is hoped, will help those directly involved to identify that knowledge for themselves. "Do it yourself!" really is the whole truth.

What is needed, then, is first a definition of collective bargaining in terms (1) of the laws and practice of the country concerned, possibly but not necessarily including some comparisons with other countries; (2) of the industry or sector in question; (3) of the rules and customs of the trade union sponsoring the course; and, finally, (4) of the collective bargaining responsibilities of the different levels of membership; in other
----

(Footnote continued from previous page)

Tools: The Use of Photographs in Workers' Education. See also Annex 4, "Further reading".

words, of their degree of participation. This final definition will lead naturally to a breakdown of the membership into the groups for which collective bargaining courses might be considered.

A definition of collective bargaining having been arrived at in this way, the subject can then be broken down into its basic elements for teaching purposes. The programme planners will then have two lists: a list of membership groups and a list of what are, in effect, teaching modules. Sections III and the two sections IV and V of this guide are an attempt at such lists, but they must not be regarded as anything more than very sketchy illustrations. The two lists having been put together, all the programme planners have to do in principle is to construct a course for any of the groups in the first list, go carefully through the second list and select what is required. That, again, is something that can only be done wisely by the persons directly involved.

Finally, when the syllabus has been hammered out, the question arises: who are to be the instructors and what teaching techniques are likely to be best for the purpose? The last section of this guide addresses itself to that question.

II. THE MEANING OF COLLECTIVE BARGAINING

As noted in the introduction, the first question programme planners must answer is: "What, for us, is the meaning of collective bargaining?" To avoid a philosophical discussion, they may find that the simplest way to approach that question is to ask another question: "What precisely are the collective bargaining activities of our union?" That question, again, can be broken down into a third set of questions: "For what purposes, on what occasions, and with whom, does the union conduct negotiations on behalf of any of its members - and which members?"

By writing down the answers to that question in a more or less systematic form - the purpose, the occasion, the members represented and the party or parties with which the bargaining takes place - the programme planners will be able to work out a definition of collective bargaining which will be immediately recognised as relevant by the union members, and to illustrate it by examples that are within the members' own experience. They will also have begun the process of dissecting the subject for teaching purposes.

Some ILO instruments (Conventions and Recommendations) deal specifically with the issue of collective bargaining. Thus Convention No. 98 defines collective bargaining as "voluntary negotiation between employers or employers' organisations and workers' organisations, with a view to the regulation of terms and conditions of employment by collective agreements". The related Recommendation No. 91 goes on to define collective agreements, in effect, as written contracts between employers' and workers' representatives. Convention No. 154 aims directly at the promotion of collective bargaining and to make collective bargaining possible for all employers and groups of workers for the purpose of determining conditions of work and employment, regulating relations between employers and workers and between employers or their organisations and workers' organisations. Recommendation No. 163 specifies the means through which collective bargaining can be promoted. (See Annex 3 for relevant texts.) The basic message contained in these instruments as well as several others is that workers shall have the right to organise and act collectively without obstruction or intimidation by the employer and that collective bargaining shall be made possible in all branches of activity. In this context it should be realised that other forms of negotiations than that when a union discusses an issue directly with an employer or employers' organisation may be described as collective bargaining.

Even in Western Europe, as Schregle has pointed out,[1] the public authorities are often brought into the process. He gives current examples from France, Norway, Belgium and Great Britain. In developing countries, government representatives are often engaged at a very early stage, in many cases, indeed, from the very beginning. Minimum wages, hours of work, annual leave entitlement,

----

[1] Johannes Schregle, "Trends in collective bargaining in Western Europe", text of a statement made at the European Conference on Labour Law and Industrial Relations, Brussels, 26-29 September 1978. Mr. Schregle is Chief of the Industrial Relations and Labour Administration Department of the ILO.

dismissal procedure, maternity and sickness benefit, pension rights
and other basic conditions of employment may be embodied in
statutory labour codes on which the final word rests with parliament
itself. In that case, a process similar to collective bargaining
really takes place with the labour department or with whatever
commission the Government may have appointed to advise it on labour
matters, and it may or may not be a tripartite process in which
representatives of the government, workers and employers sit
together at the same table at the same time to seek a consensus.

In other cases, the decision may rest with a minimum wages
board, an arbitration tribunal, an industrial court or similar
institution. It is true that the process may - or may not - begin
with direct bargaining between employers' and workers'
representatives, but even in such cases the law in many countries
provides for the very early participation of public institutions if
the sides fail to agree. In all these circumstances, the capacity
to argue a case before a more or less impartial authority, and to
argue it in terms of the national interest as well as the economics
of the industry in question, is clearly as important, or so it would
appear, as the ability to hammer out a contract with a reluctant
employer in a tough bargaining session. It is for trade unions to
decide what training their representatives require to serve their
members effectively wherever, and however, bargaining takes place.

The three phases of collective bargaining

The complete process may be considered as having three phases:
(1) formulation of the union's claims; (2) negotiations leading to
a collective agreement; (3) implementation of the agreement.

For the purposes of the present guide, we shall assume that
the third stage need present no difficulties, in principle; that any
serious infringement can be referred to the courts or other
competent authorities, or can be settled by agreed arbitration
procedures set out in the agreement itself. At a lower level,
grievance procedures for dealing with complaints of individual
members or small groups of members at the workplace will generally
be laid down in the agreement. These procedures are themselves a
form of collective bargaining. The aggrieved party may be only one
person in a particular instance, but he derives his claim from being
a member of the collective, the trade union, in whose name the
agreement was signed. Again, it is for programme planners to decide
whether to run courses in grievance handling, and if so whether to
do so as part of a wider programme concerned with collective
bargaining in the broadest sense.

In the event that the negotiators for whom the course is intended are fully conversant with the methods by which the union
arrives at an agreed set of demands, the first stage, the formulation of the statement of demands, may be passed over. Normally,
however, it can be argued that since the strongest weapon a workers'
representative can carry with him in the negotiating room is a
thorough understanding of how the claim he will be called upon to
defend was conceived, this stage should not be left out of the programme.

For the wider membership, the importance of this stage can
scarcely be exaggerated. As the persons most directly concerned,

they must be satisfied that the strongest possible claim that can cogently be defended is being advanced on their behalf. It is also the stage at which their direct participation is indispensable, at which the union's democratic machinery must be brought fully into action.

The formulation of the claim, in turn, generally falls into two distinct phases: (1) the staff work, that is the research, the statistical foundations, etc., and (2) the democratic debate and final adoption of the statement. For programme planners, the relative significance of the two phases will obviously depend on the membership group for which courses are designed.

The importance of the second phase, the union's procedural commitments, can easily be overlooked when framing courses in collective bargaining, which is too often presented as a dualogue, if not a duel, between the union's spokesmen and the "other side". Yet the workers' representatives are normally in constant close communication with their "own side" at every stage of the process, from the formulation of the claim to the final acceptance or rejection of the terms. The manner in which the membership, at different levels, participates in the process should never be left out of collective bargaining instruction.

As a rule, some kind of an instrument regulating rates of pay and conditions of work will already be in force when courses are being mounted. It may be in the form of a classical bilateral contract negotiated between independent workers' and employers' representatives, on the model of the industrialised market economies, or alternatively, a tripartite pact on which the government representatives have had, in practice, the decisive voice. In other cases the regulation may be found in a statutory labour code or parts thereof or in an industrial court ruling, etc., the contents and formulation of which the union normally has had little or no direct influence on. In yet another situation the regulating instrument may simply be an understanding at the workplace between a shop steward and management on questions best regulated at that level and incorporated in the minutes of the discussions. Even where no legal regulation or written agreement exists, where the union is embarking on the process for the very first time, there will be a complex of rules and conditons of employment established by custom or the employers' dictate, which constitute, in practice, a de facto contract. Whatever the actual situation may be the purpose of the collective bargaining process is to bring about an improvement in the existing conditions, be it either by amending the existing collective agreement or an unwritten understanding or by changes in the implementation of legal rules or by adding complementary regulations to these.

The perfect starting point

Whatever its nature, the existing agreement will provide, in the great majority of cases, the perfect starting point for a course in collective bargaining. It can be used to illustrate every detail of the process. It can be guaranteed to excite the interest - the passions, even - of the members. What, after all, is collective bargaining about? More often than not, it is about improving the existing agreement, or about its interpretation. It can hardly be about anything else.

III. TAILOR-MADE COURSES

In the planning of a training programme for union members with collective bargaining responsibilities it should be kept in mind that not every member needs to know everything that can be taught about the subject - and very few organisations would be in a position to carry out such a programme. There is a definite need for selectivity in programme composition. The expression "tailor-made course" has often been used to indicate an activity specifically designed to suit a particular group of participants selected on the basis of their need for a uniform training.

But even if the required number of all-round collective bargaining specialists is not very great, there is nevertheless one category of union representatives who should preferably possess such expertise. These are officers who lead the negotiating teams. A start might be made, therefore, by listing all the things which a perfect negotiator should understand and all the qualities he should cultivate. That itself would be an educational and stimulating operation. Sections IV and V of this guide are, in effect, an attempt at such a catalogue, but it must be emphasised again that every trade union must draw up its own list, to reflect its own unique requirements. No outsider can perform that task.

The ideal, all-inclusive list having been compiled, it can then be used as a master list when planning courses for other, less directly involved members. In each case, the relative importance of the different elements for a given membership group could be indicated in some way, perhaps by allotting a value to it, from zero up to, say, five or ten, and so a first rough formula could be noted-down quantifying the degree of attention to be given to the different elements for the intended participants. This initial formula could then serve as a basis for deciding what and how much might finally be included in the proposed course for the particular members, in the scheduled time, with the available resources.

Programme planning must be democratic

Whatever method is employed, course planning must be a democratic process with participation of representatives of the relevant group. The syllabus must respond to _their_ needs, as _they_ see them, which is not to say that advice and guidance from experienced officials will be out of place. The officials' task, however, is to stimulate the members to think frankly about their own educational needs, so that the programmes eventually mounted are really what is wanted.

A list of the main groups requiring courses from time to time might come out something like this:

(1)   rank-and-file members, especially new members;

(2)   shop-stewards, members of works councils, etc., not directly involved in negotiating agreements, though they may be concerned with implementation of the agreement at the workplace through taking up members' grievances, etc.;

(3)   branch officers and branch committee members having similar responsibilities at the branch level;

(4)   members of groups (2) and (3) with some substantive collective bargaining duties, in addition to interpretation and implementation;

(5)   members of national executives and full-time officials not directly involved in negotiating agreements, whether or not they may be called upon at times to take up with particular managements or with the public authorities questions of interpretation or implementation;

(6)   the same, with occasional substantive bargaining responsibilities, for example as lay members of negotiating teams;

(7)   full-time professionals: (a) staff employees playing a major part in preparing the statement of claim;

(8)   full-time professionals: (b) negotiators.

The above is admittedly a highly hypothetical classification for a highly hypothetical union. Only experienced officials themselves can draw up a list that is realistic for a given organisation. Programme planners, none the less, may find it a useful preliminary exercise to compile some such list, describing all the union's members in terms of the part they play in the collective bargaining process. The fact that the list will contain a specific number of groups - in the above hypothetical example, eight - does not necessarily mean, of course, that a corresponding number of separate courses are required. In practice, no doubt some of the groups can be merged, when convenient, for educational purposes. The discussion and construction of the list, however, will clarify thinking when collective bargaining courses are contemplated.

What do they need to know?

Opposite each category may be noted broadly the educational requirements of the group. If the above hypothetical classification is again used, purely for illustrative purposes, the notes could be along the following lines:

Group (1): need at least to understand the existing collective agreement* and, if it is in course of revision, enough
----

* A survey conducted in 1978 by the 90,000-strong Japan Federation of Commercial Workers' Unions (JUC) revealed that the following replies were given to the question "How much do you know about the collective labour agreement our union has achieved?" -

Know well: 5 per cent.

Know fairly well: 40 per cent.

Do not know well: 48 per cent.

Never read it: 5 per cent.

The remaining 2 per cent did not respond. No doubt a similar
(Footnote continued on next page)

of any proposed amendments to understand what the union negotiators - their representatives - are attempting and the difficulties they face; to make realistic appraisals at report-back sessions; to understand the relevant laws and union procedures and to cast their votes wisely when asked to decide whether to accept or reject an employer's offer. Similar knowledge required with respect to the formulation of a statement of claim.

Group (2): must be able to go further and explain provisions to fellow-workers, and especially to interpret clauses (in the existing agreement or under negotiation) coming within their authority, such as workplace grievance procedures and aspects of the agreement most commonly causing grievances - overtime, piece rates, bonus rights, manning, dismissal and redundancy procedures, etc. (Ask them what these issues are, in their experience.) Having daily contact with members, this group must be particularly well instructed.

Group (3): similar to shop-stewards, but since the branch may cover several enterprises a more comprehensive knowledge is required. Must be able to represent the branch, if necessary, at higher level report-back meetings on state of negotiations, and in turn to report on those meetings to the branch.

Group (4): being shop-stewards and/or branch officers, these obviously require similar courses to groups (2) and (3), plus selected or abridged parts of the courses envisaged for groups (5) to (8). If desirable, courses can concentrate on economics and other characteristics of a particular industry or area, even of a single enterprise.

Group (5): obviously need to be fully conversant with the collective bargaining process, without necessarily being skilled negotiators. They may be required to explain complex negotiations to their constituents, and sometimes to defend difficult, even unpopular decisions. Higher officers (presidents, general secretaries, etc.) will generally be members of negotiating teams and hence belong to group (6) or group (8).

Group (6): as group (5), plus selected or abridged parts of courses prepared for group (8).

Group (7): need a specialised facility in labour economics, law, statistics, etc. If the union is in a position to employ a sufficient staff, these officals can no doubt be recruited in the first place from universities and other institutions of higher learning, including labour colleges where they exist. Otherwise, the union may have to mount its own courses, possibly in conjunction with other unions or federations. In any event, some

----

(Footnote continued from previous page)

inquiry in other unions in other countries would yield not very different results.

additional training in the problems of the particular industry or sector and in the union's policy and procedures will generally be useful.

Group (8): clearly need a comprehensive knowledge of the entire collective bargaining process, including a thorough understanding of the technical work done by the members of group (7), without necessarily being themselves experts; in other words, they must be capable of fully mastering a brief. They must also, of course, be persuasive advocates and skilled negotiators.

In addition to broadly conceived courses in the collective bargaining process, more or less covering the above ground according to the different membership levels, there may well be a demand for enlightenment on particular aspects of the subject. Branch members, for example, may be puzzled by the statistics used, both by the union and by management, while having in other respects an adequate understanding of what is happening. Two or three sessions, or even a single exposition at a branch meeting, may then be arranged on that aspect. Shop-stewards may feel they should know more about economic developments in the industry in which they work, so as to represent their fellow-workers more confidently in meetings with management, or they may require instruction in new or proposed methods of wage determination, incentive schemes, productivity deals and so on. At the other end of the involvement scale, top-level negotiators themselves may feel they are weak on a particular aspect and would benefit from a special course.

In all cases, the obvious way to ascertain what special courses are required is to ask the members concerned. Run quickly through the major elements in the collective bargaining process, and inquire whether there are any on which further enlightenment would be welcome. That, again, does not mean that officials are debarred from throwing in a few suggestions. Consultation is essential if courses are to meet the members' needs.

IV. TEACHING MODULES: THE COLLECTIVE AGREEMENT

The detailed construction of a syllabus for a collective bargaining course, at whatever level, will be greatly facilitated if the subject as a whole has first been broken down into relatively small modules, each of which can be taught separately, if desired, or a number of which can be selected and combined to fit the specific requirements of a given membership group. Modules can, of course, be continually partitioned to form smaller modules: it is for the people directly involved to decide just what constitutes for them a convenient, compact parcel of knowledge which may be wrapped up and delivered, so to speak, in one handy piece, to be consumed on its own, or on other occasions tied together in a package with other pieces.

The fact that a particular component of a syllabus has been isolated in that way does not necessarily imply that teaching it will require a full session. Part of a session may suffice, or on the other hand more than one session may be needed. In any event, it will depend partly on the learning capacity of the participants. The underlying principle is rather like that of a construction toy: if the player has a full set of all the necessary pieces, he can put together a very simple artifact using just a few of the pieces, or he can assemble an elaborate structure using most or all of the pieces, and he can progress from one to the other. The important thing is to have a selection of pieces available which have been carefully shaped for their purpose, so as to simplify the execution of the intended design, whatever its degree of complexity.

Ideally, each module should be a self-contained unit, with its own teaching kit and panel of instructors or discussion leaders who can be drawn on to take that part of the course. In workers' education, however, many of the latter will not be professional teachers but union officials whose task, in part at least, is to communicate their personal experience. Such individuals, obviously, must be encouraged to introduce their own illustrative material wherever possible.

Two convenient stages

Collective bargaining might conveniently be taught in two stages: (1) the collective agreement; (2) the collective bargaining process.

By the collective agreement is meant simply the document itself, how it came to be formulated and the provisions embodied in it for its interpretation and enforcement, including the members' involvement at every stage. The second phase would deal with the actual negotiating of the agreement, from the presentation of the union's proposals to the final signing of the accepted terms, again including the members' participation in the situation as it develops. The first phase - the collective agreement - might stand by itself as a separate, complete course, but the second phase would normally follow on the first, or at least on selected parts of the first.

In both phases it will generally be found advisable to stick to an existing agreement - what it is, how it works and how it was negotiated - rather than broach the highly controversial issues raised by a current claim. Otherwise, the educational sessions can easily become a series of heated debates on aspects of union policy. The place for such debates is at branch meetings and similar gatherings, as part of the members' involvement in the collective bargaining process. Even where such a meeting has been specially called to explain some aspect of a current claim, that meeting is part of the process itself, not of teaching the process.

It is true that participation is a very educational experience - quite possibly, for certain matters, the best form of education - and this is recognised later in this guide; but where the member is simply participating at a conventional union meeting, exercising his constitutional right to do so, the meeting would not normally be regarded as part of the union's educational programme, even though members of the union's teaching team might have been called upon to assist.

That said, it must be conceded that if a collective bargaining course happens to be in progress when a new claim is being formulated or negotiated it will be very difficult to keep all mention of the details out of the lecture room. In those circumstances, it must be left to the course leader's judgement to decide in what way the current claim can be introduced for illustrative purposes, and to close the subject tactfully when discussion, encouraged for the purpose of clarification, begins to turn into a debate on union policy. Similarly, it is for the participants in the course to understand and accept its true purpose, with the limitations unavoidably imposed in consequence on what otherwise they might consider their right to free speech. That right, as the course leader no doubt will emphasise, can be fully aired at the proper time and place.

The collective agreement: a possible breakdown

The first stage of the course - the collective agreement - might be broken down as follows.

1.   Your collective agreement

The present agreement (or agreements) of direct interest to the participants, broadly described. If the course is concerned only with the content of the agreement, proceed direct to No. 4.

2.   The legal framework

The laws governing collective bargaining; statutory labour code, if any; status of agreement in law; use of courts and other legal institutions for interpretation and enforcement; legal penalties, if any, that can be imposed for infringements. Note that at this stage we are concerned with the legal framework of the agreement as such. Statutory conciliation and arbitration facilities for resolving difficulties in reaching the agreement, where they exist, belong to the second stage, the bargaining process.

3.   The statement of claim

How the union agrees upon proposals for a new agreement;   its
democratic procedures for so doing; the staff work involved;
balancing the members' legitimate objectives with employers' (and
possibly the national economy's) capacity to pay; hence exact cost
of each item to be calculated; the basic justification   for
proposals, on broad social and economic grounds; the problem of
priorities - wages, hours, leave, pensions, etc. - concentrate on
one or two, or go for a package?

4.   Wages, working time

Clauses dealing with wages, hours, annual leave, etc.,
including compensation due on dismissal. The underlying statistics.

5.   Pensions

Clauses dealing with various pension rights, provident funds,
etc. The underlying statistics.

6.   Social benefits

Sick leave, maternity leave, etc. and related payments. The
underlying statistics. (Note: the employer's legal responsibility
for workman's compensation to be mentioned here if No. 2 has been
skipped.)

7.   Fringe benefits

Any other benefits provided for in the agreement, not coming
under the above major headings; for example, travel allowances,
housing allowances of various kinds, leave of absence and grants (if
any) for family occasions such as marriages, betrothels, funerals,
etc. The underlying statistics.

8.   Sources of information

The principal sources of major statistics and other important
information relevant to the agreement: cost-of-living statistics,
wages trends, company profits and dividend distribution (i.e.
national trends and trends in particular industries and economic
sectors, not individual companies at this stage);   the gross
national product; distribution of the national income, etc. Where
there is a good financial press, do not overlook this as a source of
information. Statements of leading financiers, company directors,
government spokesmen, etc. can be very revealing.

9.   Company accounts (where relevant)

Define limited liability and other types of company, if
relevant.   Information they are required by law to publish. Where
and how to obtain that information. How to read a profit-and-loss
account and a balance sheet: what in particular to extract for

collective bargaining purposes. Again do not ignore the financial press, in which the company's annual meeting and directors' report, with the chairman's supporting statement, may well be fully reported.

10.   Non-economic clauses

Dismissal and redundancy procedures, the employer's rights, the workers' rights. Provisions for union consultation and participation in these and other fields. Conditions for terminating the agreement and for initiating negotiations for a revised agreement.

11.   Interpretation and application

Grievance procedures; provisions for settling differences arising over application of the agreement or questions outside the agreement (i.e. procedures laid down in the agreement, not its enforcement at law; but if No. 2 has been skipped, the legal status of the agreement can be indicated).

Finally, it must be emphasised again that only programme planners with an actual collective agreement in front of them can break the subject down into suitable teaching components; also that the modules can be used alone, can be combined or condensed, or divided still further. The legal framework, for example, could easily be expanded into several lectures for members or officials wishing to make a more thorough study of that subject, with item No. 18 from the next section added. Items 4 to 7 could be condensed into a single session for members needing only to grasp the underlying statistics of collective bargaining well enough to understand what is entailed in putting together a well-founded set of demands. On the other hand, left as they are, or even developed further, these items could form the basis for a separate specialist course in the statistics of collective bargaining. The sole purpose of the above list is to help programme planners compile their own lists.

The second part of the course - the bargaining process - is dealt with in the following chapter.

V. TEACHING MODULES: THE BARGAINING PROCESS

Most of the points emphasised in connection with the collective agreement apply with even greater force to the teaching of the collective bargaining process. Only those who have actually and if possible repeatedly taken part in negotiations and have done so moreover in the relevant economic sector, can give reliable advice on what needs to be taught to a given group of union members - always in consultation, of course, with the members concerned. In some instances, negotiations are fairly quickly completed; in others, they may be protracted for weeks, if not months. In some, the atmosphere may normally be rather tense, at least at the beginning; in others, it may be relatively cordial; in others judicial, and the negotiators' psychological approach will be affected accordingly.

One must assume, however, that in all cases collective bargaining consists essentially in the union representatives arguing a case with the employers' representatives, whether they do so directly with no other parties present, or with the participation of a third party whose role is to conciliate, reconcile and possibly exercise a casting vote, or with the two sides appearing in turn before a third party or a tribunal whose members ask questions suggested by their own experience or by the points already made to them by the "other side", before eventually making a ruling. In this last case, the union representatives are really debating against an absent opponent, but they are debating none the less. They ought to have a pretty good idea of the opponent's position, his strengths and weaknesses, must anticipate the replies he will make to their own case, and may well have been permitted to study any written statements he has submitted.

In this guide, we shall assume that negotiations take place direct between the two sides, and programme planners will have to make the necessary adjustments if that is not the way collective bargaining normally begins in their country. The two great essentials - a good case and the capacity to defend it - are in any event common to all the different procedures for reaching an agreement.

At this stage of the course, it must be assumed that participants have already been through the first stage, the collective agreement, or through sufficient parts of it to prepare them for a study of the bargaining process itself. It is assumed that the statement of claim has been adopted, and that every item in it can be backed by fact and reason. So far, no one outside the union has been involved. Now, with the exposure of the union's case to critical, possibly hostile examination, a totally new phase begins.

For workers' educational purposes, the collective bargaining process might very tentatively be divided more or less into the following elements. (The numbering continues from the previous section, since for certain courses education officers might wish to combine portions from both sections).

12.   The collective bargaining process

A straightforward description of the relevant process, which can stand on its own or serve as an introduction to a longer course. Emphasise, again, the members' participation in the process.

13.   The opening statement

The employers have agreed to negotiate, have presumably received a statement of claim in writing and a first meeting has been arranged. The union carefully chooses its delegation, which ideally will include specialists in the different major clauses of the draft. The leader of the delegation makes an opening submission, broadly stating the union's case on general social and economic grounds without at this stage entering into statistical detail. The management representatives may then make brief general observations, also without coming to close grips; they will normally undertake to give the union's demands serious study and to offer a considered reply at an early date. Union representatives suggest that a reply in writing would facilitate negotiations at the next meeting. A date is fixed, or a procedure agreed upon for calling that meeting.

14.   Proposals and counter-proposals

Employers' reply received and analysed; arguments and counter-proposals carefully rehearsed. Questions of priorities again - readiness to compromise on certain items so as to justify firmness on others. Negotiations resumed. Management representatives may wish to speak first, elaborating on their written reply; obviously that is for them to decide. Union leader replies to employers' case, probably negatively at first, simply repudiating major theme; other delegation members come in on appropriate items. Compromise, however, is offered, either at end of speech or when pressed by employers. It is now employers' turn to reply and to be pressed in their turn to make concrete proposals.

The cycle of proposals followed by counter-proposals continues until a formula acceptable to both sides has been reached. The complete process may require several meetings, but the technique of each cycle is much the same. Again emphasise very strongly consultation and contact with membership throughout, especially final procedure for acceptance or rejection of the terms.

15.   Negotiating techniques

No substitute for thorough preparation of good case. Most important technique, that of lucid exposition, already indicated. The rest is largely a matter of tactics. Certain major points may well be emphasised. For example:

(a)   self-confidence is all important, especially where union representatives may be at an educational disadvantage, lack experience or might allow themselves, for historical or cultural reasons, to be overawed in the presence of "authority". Must establish equality of status at the outset, assert the same "authority" as the employers;

(b)   at the same time, be always courteous;

(c)   all members of negotiating team should participate from time
        to time, with evident expertise: this is desirable in itself
        and also helps to convey that impression of authority. Except
        possibly at initial meeting, where in any case they will all
        be introduced, no persons should attend who are going to be
        mute, unless it is clearly understood that they have been
        invited as observers, whose silence will be accepted and
        appreciated;

(d)   the consultation of technical advisers who are not actually
        delegation members should not be made in front of the opposite
        party - apart from an occasional passing of a written note to
        the chairman of the delegation. Such consultations should
        take place during adjournments at which time the issues may be
        thoroughly examined without the risk of disclosing uncertainty
        or divided views to the other side.

(e)   representatives should not allow themselves to be disconcerted
        by an argument they have not anticipated or by the sudden
        injection of new matter or unexpected counter-proposals; they
        should calmly ask for an adjournment to study the new
        development, if necessary long enough to consult the union
        executive or other appropriate membership;

(f)   sources which cannot be checked should not be introduced by
        either side. If management cites a report that is not
        available to the public or has not been made available to the
        union, the workers' representatives should assert their right
        to see a copy if it is to be used in argument. They can then
        study it and evaluate its worth;

(g)   they should always insist that they are answerable to the
        members; it is no diminutation of their authority - quite the
        reverse - to emphasise their representative status; to
        impress the "other side" with the strength of the members'
        feelings, with the fact that the union leaders have to carry
        the members with them if an agreement is to be concluded;

(h)   above all, they should try always to keep the initiative.

16.   The information service

        Not to be confused with the union's constitutional procedures
for member participation, which will have been covered, in passing,
under other items, but includes information to members through
circulars, the union journal, etc. and to other unions where
desirable. Contacts with the media: press statements, press
conferences, etc. Role of public opinion: can be exaggerated, but
public sympathy can be useful, hostile opinion harmful, especially
where "other side" has made an issue of effect on consumer prices.
Press statements sometimes made for benefit of members, who receive
quick information this way.

        Note that the aim of public information service is to explain
the union's position, not to continue the debate in public. The
employers, naturally, may also put out statements, also to make
their position clear to the public; but the place for the give-and-

take of collective bargaining is the relevant negotiating forum.
Any joint statements explaining state of negotiations or conclusion
of agreement must be seen and approved by both sides. Much
annoyance and misunderstanding can be caused by assuming they are a
formality which may be left to one side or the other - usually to
the employers, who generally have better staff facilities.

17. Resolving_a_deadlock

If reached at meeting, propose adjournment to consult members.
Assumption must be that employers have made their "final" offer and
that this is unacceptable to the union negotiators; otherwise the
process of proposal and counter-proposal can continue. Members
asked to give clear "yes" or "no" on employers' offer. Again
emphasise union's procedures for obtaining this decision, the role
of the union executive (or other appropriate authority) in providing
guidance, etc. If answer is "no", offer to resume negotiations. If
these are refused, or serve only to confirm the deadlock, proceed
according to the union's rules and custom, any mutually agreed
arbitration procedures and the law of the land. Explain these.

(Note: the aim of other measures the union may take to
enforce its claim - demonstrations, withdrawal of labour, etc. - is
the resumption of the collective bargaining process, not part of the
process, and hence outside the scope of the present guide. Hints
that demands for such action, if within the law, might be difficult
to resist, are, of course, part of the legitimate tactics of
collective bargaining, but such action itself is not negotiation.)

18. Legal_conciliation_and_arbitration

What the law provides in this respect, treated at greater
length. How to make the best use of these facilities.

Essential_elements

It will be quite evident that the above analysis is based on
a purely hypothetical bargaining process, against an equally
hypothetical background. In a guide of this sort, intended for use
in a number of different countries, it could hardly be otherwise.
None the less, whatever the machinery for determining conditions of
employment, the process will generally be found to consist of three
essential elements, which might be called the beginning, the middle
and the end:

(1)   the presentation of the union's case; that is, an opening
      statement;

(2)   a debate of some sort;

(3)   the conclusion; that is, the procedure for reaching or
      obtaining a decision.

If programme planners will concentrate on these three elements, they
should be able to break down the collective bargaining process for
teaching purposes into units that will fit their union's unique
requirements.

VI. TEACHING METHODS AND TECHNIQUES: SOME GENERAL OBSERVATIONS

Four general points might be borne in mind before teaching methods are considered in detail.

The first is that there is no effective substitute for a good teacher with real experience of the subject. By "good" in this context is meant simply a person with an aptitude for communicating experience to the type of people who take part in trade union courses. That aptitude may be cultivated by practice, and if the practitioner is able to study some simple basic teaching techniques, including the utilisation of the kind of teaching aids that might be available, so much the better. But first-hand experience of the subject to be taught is all-important, especially where it involves human relations, such as bargaining with an employer, appearing before a tribunal, hammering out a statement of claim or participating in the union's democratic decision-making procedures.

Even a technical subject like statistics is better taught, to a trade union class, by labour statisticians who have practical experience of working on collective agreements. Similarly with labour law. Experts with a purely academic knowledge of a subject, or whose experience does not include major labour aspects, will almost certainly run into difficulties with a trade union class when the time comes for questions and discussion.

There are really two kinds of experience that are valuable: experience of the subject and experience of teaching the subject. The paramount importance of the first derives not only from the fact that practical experience, in many contexts, is the only way to obtain a thorough knowledge of the subject; it flows also from the psychology of an adult workers' class. The participants will almost always prefer to learn about a subject from a trade union expert, preferably one of their own officials, even if he is not a very good communicator, than from a professional teacher however brilliant. For one thing, they feel they are receiving from their fellow trade unionist the knowledge they believe is really practical and useful to them. For another, they are given from the start a sense of equality; they do not feel they are being treated as children who have been sent back to school. This reassurance is not only satisfying in itself; it helps to break down the barrier between teacher and taught and to encourage the participation of the latter in the educational process. The word "participant", so often used in connection with workers' education, is not a mere euphemism for "student".

The more practical experience of the subject the lecturer has, the more his contribution will be appreciated. If the union's top negotiator is brought in as a guest speaker, the members will be gratified, even if he has had little time to prepare his material and is not a born teacher. Any defects he may have in that respect will be offset by his deep knowledge of the subject, and the members will certainly know how to take advantage of that. Many a poor lecture has been turned into a first-rate educational experience by the pertinent questions and discussion of the participants. Always leave plenty of time for them!

A panel of available talent

The union's education officer should draw up a panel of experienced officials who are willing to lecture or to act as discussion leaders on different aspects of collective bargaining. If the union's resources run to the employment of some full-time paid lecturers, well and good, but the point underlined above about experience is still valid. Ideally, they should be trade union officials turned teachers, not vice versa. If the time can be found, all regular panel members should attend a short practical course in workers' education methods and techniques.

Depending on the size of the union, a second "guest" panel might be added, of prominent leaders who might be available from time to time but who would not be expected to take on educational activity as a normal part of their official duties. If willing to co-operate, certain independent experts with the requisite experience - the president of an industrial court, for example, or a labour department conciliator - might constitute a third list.

Learning by experience

The second general observation also concerns experience, but not the teacher's experience. It concerns, rather, the possibility of teaching the subject, to some degree, by experience. Obviously, union members will learn much about the union's own procedures by taking part in them, at the level where it is constitutionally proper for them to do so. Equally obviously, course leaders will urge participants to play their full part in the union's normal procedures, for educational as well as more basic reasons. That, however, is not organised educational activity. At other levels, for edcuational purposes, participants in collective bargaining courses might be permitted to attend relevant meetings - sittings of the national executive, for example - as observers. They would not be allowed to contribute, but they would make copious notes and would hold a thorough discussion of the proceedings at a later session of their own, with the guidance of the group leader.

Similarly, permission might be obtained for them to attend, as observers, some of the bargaining sessions with the employers, meetings of arbitration tribunals, industrial courts and so on. In all cases, in the ensuing educational session, it would be for the group leader to guide the discussion in such a way that the members concentrated on the procedures they had witnessed, without becoming too engrossed in the substance of the case.

None of this, obviously, would be possible if no part of the collective bargaining process was occurring at the same time as a trade union course. When there was no course in progress at the opportune time, however, permission might still be sought for selected union members to attend certain sessions as observers, for the educational experience, and to hold a discussion on the proceedings afterwards. The occasion might be used to stimulate interest in a more formal collective bargaining course to be organised at a later date. Whether some such arrangements are feasible will depend on the circumstances of the particular union in the particular country. The suggestion is made here for what it may be worth.

Some participants may well have a certain personal experience of the collective bargaining process, from previous occasions when claims were being pressed or in connection with the implementation of the existing agreement. A good lecturer will make sure that such experience is brought out and made use of for teaching purposes. This is a matter of teaching techniques and will be referred to again later in this guide.

Experience is such a good teacher that a lot of educational mileage can be obtained by simulating experience, where real experience is out of reach. Various possibilities for doing so are also discussed later in this guide.

Teaching equipment: keep it simple

The third general point concerns teaching equipment. Because trade union educators are not normally professional teachers, there is a tendency at times for them to exaggerate a little the value of the apparatus employed in present-day schools and colleges and to be overawed by the apparent difficulty of acquiring the modern teacher's skills. Trade union educators, however, start with the enormous advantage that the men and women who join their courses do so because they really want to learn about the subject for its own sake; they come along with a pretty good general impression of what it is all about, and the lecturer's task in a collective bargaining course, as noted above, is usually to pass on to them the lessons of his own experience. He should be able to do that without a lot of expensive equipment and without recourse to methods of teaching that are intended for full-time professionals.

In this guide, only teaching equipment will be recommended that is within the means of a relatively small union, and only teaching techniques will be proposed that are within the capabilities of a typical, well-intentioned, efficient trade union official.

Make frequent progress checks

The fourth general point is that, as with all workers' education activities, a frank exchange of views should be held at appropriate times on the progress of the course, to confirm that all concerned are satisfied that it is attaining its objectives. For a short course, this discussion can take the form of an evaluation session when the course is over, in which case the lessons learned will be applied to subsequent courses. For longer courses, discussions can be held at suitable intervals, perhaps by allotting a certain time for the purpose towards the end of some of the regular sessions. This may not be a teaching technique in the strict sense, but it has an obvious bearing on teaching techniques and it helps to establish the character of the course as a co-operative effort in which all are treated as equals.

VII. TEACHING EQUIPMENT AND MATERIAL

As already noted, several excellent publications exist for the trade union official wishing to study the techniques of workers' education.[1] Equipment and material may be divided broadly into two categories: (1) those used by the teacher himself, and generally only by him; (2) those distributed to the participants or which they may be assumed to possess or be able to obtain.

Since nearly all knowledge is communicated by either sight or sound, material teaching aids will generally be either something to look at or something to listen to. The exception is where skill in mastering a physical tool of some sort has to be acquired - operating a typewriter, for example; in which case, practice with the tool itself is essential. In collective bargaining, there are not normally any tools of that sort to worry about, but there is one possible exception which may be mentioned at this stage.

The pocket electronic calculator is now so inexpensive and so universally available that some practice in its operation might be included in certain courses if it is generally agreed that to do so would be valuable. Obviously, participants need to know how to work out relevant calculations in the old-fashioned way to begin with, in order to understand thoroughly the underlying mathematics, but once they have acquired that facility the advantages of being able to perform the same calculation swiftly with the aid of a mini-computer need hardly be stressed. Even across the negotiating table, union representatives often find it helpful to make a few fast calculations when statistics are being bandied about. Whether to bring pocket calculators into certain parts of a collective bargaining course is, again, something only programme planners can decide. If so, the instruments should all be basically of the same design.

How we absorb information

Recent research into how adults generally absorb information during their daily lives shows that, very roughly, 75 per cent is received through sight, 12.5 per cent through hearing and the remaining 12.5 per cent through the other senses of smell, taste and touch.[2] If for our present purpose we can eliminate smell, taste and touch, that would leave sight with 86 per cent and sound with 14 per cent. Further research into the amount of information actually retained by adult students when communicated by different methods produced the following results:

Ears only: 20 per cent retained.

Eyes only: 30 per cent retained.

Ears + eyes: 50 per cent retained.

----

[1] See Annex 4, "Further reading".

[2] These and other statistics in this paragraph are from the ILO Manual, "Workers' Education and its Techniques".

Ears + eyes + discussion: 70 per cent retained.

Ears + eyes + discussion + practice: 90 per cent retained.

One of the evident conclusions to be drawn from these figures
is that the most useful material aids to teaching any subject will
be visual ones, or possibly audio-visual. Most of the required
sound can be produced by that ancient device, the Adam's Apple;   in
other words, by the voices of lecturers and participants. Only one
purely sound appliance within reach of the average union is likely
to be of some limited assistance, and that is the tape-recorder.

Use of the tape-recorder

Where a class has been divided into small groups to meet
separately (for case analyses or role-playing, for example) it might
sometimes be interesting to record the separate discussions and play
them back, in whole or selected parts, for the benefit of the
reassembled class. This might be particularly instructive where the
different groups have been required to study the same case and have
come up with varying conclusions. Further, permission might be
obtained to make recordings of some actual bargaining sessions or
arbitration hearings - for example, the opening meeting at which the
leader of the union team presents the union case and other crucial
stages.

In some countries, all proceedings are taped in any event for
the purpose of obtaining a reliable record, and in such cases copies
of some of the tapes might be procured. Played back to a collective
bargaining class, this material would undoutedly be highly
instructive, but it would have to be carefully edited (not censored)
beforehand, so that selected passages could be introduced by the
instructor and discussed by the participants.   Since collective
bargaining is essentially a debate, audial teaching techniques have
an obvious appeal.

A "set-piece", such as the union leader's opening statement,
could indeed be recorded in the union's office if need be, so that
the main characteristics could be noted: the courteous opening
remarks, the introduction of the other team members, the
presentation of the main theme, the use of broad supporting
arguments and facts, the definition of the claims, a mention of the
union members' expectations, the simplicity and clarity of the
exposition, avoidance of rhetoric, the firmness and effectiveness of
the closing sentences, etc.

Some participants may possess their own cassette recorders and
may wish to record some of the course. There is no reason why they
should not be allowed to do so, since they and their friends may
enjoy the play-back and it will have the educational value of
repetition. This is really a form of note-taking, however.   The
cassette is no substitute for the good old-fashioned notebook (on
which some comments are made below) but it can be a very useful
adjunct to the notebook because of its completeness and accuracy.
The owner of a tape-recorder can use it to confirm, fill in, clarify
and expand his notes when he finds these are not satisfactory, as we
all do at times.

Instructors themselves may wish to record certain sessions of
a course, if only to check on their own performance or to pick out

points for future emphasis or discussion. That is not the same, however, as using the tape-recorder for teaching purposes as such.

The blackboard above all

What of the all-important visual aids which may be used by the teacher? The best and cheapest is still the oldest, the blackboard or chalkboard. The purpose of the blackboard is to display information, so that the learners may absorb it through their eyes, and also, if they wish, copy it into their notebooks. The purpose of all the more sophisticated display techniques - the flipcharts, flannel boards, overhead projectors, film strips, and the like - is really essentially the same. This is not said to deride the use of these devices, but rather to encourage the trade union teacher to cultivate a good blackboard technique above all.

The advantage of the other devices is that they can be professionally or semi-professionally produced and once made they can be carried about from place to place and used countless times. They thus ensure a certain standard. They also have the appeal of novelty and variety, thereby helping to stimulate attention. In fact, with a little familiarity, they are easier to use than the blackboard.

The blackboard, on the other hand, can be more dynamic and it reflects the personality of the lecturer. He can write onto it anything he particularly wishes the participants to remember. He can build up a certain suspense, by developing illustrations by stages. For example, he can construct a chart level by level, piece by piece, or point by point. He can reveal the process by which the ideas of a rank-and-file member may finally reach the negotiating chamber or an industrial court, to be incorporated perhaps in a new collective agreement, by indicating the steps progressively, one by one; and he can illustrate the reverse process, the report-back provisions, in a similar way. He can indicate movement by means of arrows pointing this way or that. He can make simple pictures, such as a ladder to suggest the concept of steps for climbing or descending, drawing in the steps one by one and writing labels against them. With a little practice, he will have no difficulty in representing human beings in some simplified way such as the familiar "matchstick" figures.

In explaining statistics the blackboard can be used to show how a given conclusion is arrived at step by step, and this can be done as slowly or as rapidly as the participants can keep up with the demonstration. The lecturer can also dismantle an illustration piece by piece by rubbing out parts that are no longer relevant, such as processes that have been completed or are out-dated, persons who have been dismissed from office or otherwise eliminated from the proceedings, fallacies which have been exposed, calculations that have been proved inaccurate...

At all times, the lecturer who is at home with his blackboard can enlist the co-operation of the class in a way that is more direct and spontaneous than with other forms of display. He can invite them to tell him from their own experience what is the next point he should note on the board, and he can suggest that one or other of them comes forward to do the job himself. He can even make deliberate mistakes, to test the alertness of the participants, to

break down tension and to introduce a bit of fun into what is often
a solemn affair. Even a simple spelling error has been known to
achieve that end.

The overhead projector

Of the more sophisticated visual aids, the one most likely to
be useful in teaching collective bargaining, if the union can obtain
one, is probably the overhead projector, or an old-fashioned
epidiascope. Either of these will permit documents to be projected
onto a screen large enough for all to read. A clause of the
collective agreement, for example, on which the lecturer wishes to
place particular emphasis and to hold a fairly lengthy discussion,
can be displayed in this way. Similarly, a cumbersome table of
statistics, or a chart too complex to be built up easily on the
blackboard, can be screened.

In all such cases, photocopies of the documents should also be
distributed to the class, unless there is some overriding reason why
this is undesirable. During the teaching session, however, it will
be pleasanter for the participants and more of a communal experience
to look at the material on the screen, and it will be easier for the
lecturer to identify parts to which he wishes to draw attention.
The overhead projector will also enable him to do some of the things
he does on the blackboard, since it can screen his own handiwork,
but a lecturer can never have the same living relationship with a
machine that he has with a blackboard and some coloured chalks.

It must be remembered also that most projection techniques
require the room to be in darkness or semi-darkness, and that tends
to cut everybody off from everybody else, as well as inhibiting
notetaking and perhaps even inducing somnolence. It is for all
concerned to weigh the relative advantages of alternative
techniques.

You can make your own slides

One sophisticated projection technique will generally be
within the capacity of the average small union. There will nearly
always be at least one member who is a skilful amateur photographer
with a 35 mm camera and the requisite slide projector. The sort of
pictures often used in collective bargaining manuals, showing
members and others taking part in meetings of various sorts, can be
posed and made into slides, or permission can be obtained for
photographing actual occasions for this purpose. With a good 35 mm
camera, moreover, there should be no difficulty in reproducing
documents quite sharp enough for teaching purposes, so obtaining
some of the benefits for which otherwise an overhead projector would
be required.

At a slightly more sophisticated level, the slides can be made
into film strips and a strip projector or adaptor used. In either
case, the officials concerned should get together and work out a
suitable scenario to depict the collective bargaining process,
preferably before the pictures are taken, so that a screen show of
reasonable length and completeness can be given. A collection of
three or four slides would obviously be more trouble than they are
worth. An accompanying text, briefly identifying each frame, should

be provided, but lecturers must be encouraged to make their own commentary, never just reading from a prepared script, and always bringing in their own experience when relevant.

Some of the better frames can be blown up and placed on permanent display during the course. A wall display of this sort can be helpful in giving the participants something to look at and discuss during coffeebreaks, as well as helping to communicate some useful knowledge. If photographs on display are in fact the same as those used in a slide show, there is something to be said for postponing the permanent exhibition until after the screening has taken place. This will increase the curiosity of the participants in the pictures when they are displayed, as well as avoiding a feeling of repetition when the slides are being screened.

Text books and memory aids

Of the visual material available to the participants themselves, the most common are three in number: text books, documents of various sorts distributed during or after a teaching session by the lecturer, and the participant's own note book. It will be observed that these three are in reality all the same device in principle: they are printed or written material which the participant can take away, to look at and absorb in private in his own time, at his own pace.

Text books can be publications or manuals of a relatively high academic standard, or quite simple home-made pamphlets prepared for a particular group of workers and either printed inexpensively or reproduced on the union's duplicating machine. Examples are the text entitled "Collective Bargaining" produced for the ILO/DANIDA Caribbean Workers' Education Project and the booklet "Why Collective Bargaining?" published by the Central Board for Workers' Education in India, but there are many others.[1]

Whatever type of text book is used, it is important that the educational sessions and the text book study are kept in phase; in other words, that the participants should not be expected to read, in earnest, parts of the book that do not correspond to what has been taught so far in the class. If fast learners wish to race ahead with their reading, well and good, but they should not be allowed to disrupt the orderly development of the course by raising points scheduled for treatment in later sessions. A comparatively short, simple text might, of course, be read once in its entirety by participants before or at the beginning of a course, but detailed study, backed by a second reading, should proceed as a general rule by stages. Some of the simpler texts, in any event, are intended to be covered completely in a single session.

Material distributed by the lecturer will include (a) documents required to illustrate his comments and stimulate discussion during the session, such as copies of the collective agreement itself and of relevant charts and statistical tables, and (b) documents issued at the end of the session as an aide-mémoire. The latter might include a summary of the ground covered by each session. In all cases, documents should if possible be on standard-size sheets ready punched for insertion in a loose-leaf binder, together with the participant's own notes.
----

[1] See Annex 4, "Further reading".

The distribution of the second type of document - the memory aid - will be most valuable where participants have limited practice of note taking, as is frequently the case in workers' education, and it will be appreciated even by experienced students. None the less, no mass-produced material, however good, can totally replace notes made by the participant, who is conscious of his individual needs and recognises the points he particularly wants to remember. Recognising this, and understanding that many of his listeners may not be very good at taking notes, the considerate speaker will present his material in such a way as to facilitate note taking.

He will write on the board any phrase or fact of which he considers it essential the participants should take note, and will allow time for them to do so without appearing to be waiting for them or giving dictation. At the same time, if he intends to distribute a relevant document at the end of the session, he can say, "There is no need to copy this down in detail; I will give you a copy later." Sighs of relief all round!

The aim should be a compendium of information compiled by the participant himself from the various sources, under the guidance of a tutor but still the worker's own creation, in which he can take a proper pride.

VIII. SOME TEACHING TECHNIQUES: LISTENING AND TALKING

Teaching techniques have unavoidably been discussed to some extent in previous sections. In this and the following section, some three or four of the more useful techniques will be described, with suggestions for their application in collective bargaining courses.

Whatever technique is selected for a given subject, the figures quoted in the previous section indicate that, if at all possible, the person responsible should aim at a combination of sight, sound, discussion and practice in every session: what might be called the SSDP formula. The only one of these which may have to be omitted from a given session, through lack of time, is the last, practice, but this can be amply rectified in later sessions unless the course is a very short one indeed.

It will be observed that the last two factors, discussion and practice, entail the direct participation of the members, but it must not be assumed that participation is necessarily absent from the other two. The sound need not always be the sound of a lecturer's voice, nor the sight that of the lecturer's artifacts. The aim should be the greatest practicable degree of member participation at all times. In fact, if a single word were required to identify the essential characteristic of good workers' education, it would be: participation.

The one-man lecture

The SSDP formula should be borne in mind above all when preparing material for the first of the teaching techniques still most commonly used in workers' education: the simple one-man lecture. However complete his mastery of the subject, the lecturer who addresses his class for 45 minutes without pausing will almost certainly fail to communicate effectively, as well as quite possibly offending his listeners if they are union members. Fortunately, few lecturers do that these days - they at least write a few more or less legible figures on the blackboard - but many still rely far too much on their own unaided powers of speech.

The four desirable elements - sound, sight, discussion and practice - need not be introduced one after the other like sequences in a four-act play. On the contrary, the first three at least should be continuously interacting, and the alert lecturer will be guiding the session with this process in mind. For example, if he is to lecture on the existing collective agreement - the item 1 of our suggested breakdown - the first thing he will do is announce the subject (sound). He will then write the formal title of the lecture on the blackboard (sight). At that point, the members will probably write the phrase in their notebooks (sight with an element of participation).

He may then wish to point out that the first things to note about any collective agreement are the parties who are bound by it, the date it came into force and its intended duration. Again, he can then simply give all that information by word of mouth (sound), write it on the board (sight), and the members no doubt will again copy the matter into their notebooks. On the other hand, before he confirms the information himself, he can ask if any one can say who are the parties to the agreement. Several members no doubt will be able to give the correct answer to that question, which will generally be simply the name of the union and the name of the company, or the employers' association.

Similarly, he can ask if anyone can give the relevant dates, and with a little coaxing he may get several answers to that rather more difficult question. He writes them all on the board, comments on them if any comment is appropriate, maybe asks the different contributors why they believe in the dates they have given and finally gives the correct answer. He then rubs out all the others. Never leave anything inaccurate on display for more than a few minutes!

In this way, right at the outset, the lecturer has employed sound, sight and an element of discussion, and has enlisted the co-operation of the participants. They are "in on the act" from the beginning. He can then ask what exactly is meant by "collective agreement" and when he has guided the ensuing discussion to an acceptable definition that, too, can be written on the board for all to see. At some point during this early stage he will distribute copies of the agreement, politely asking one of the members to hand them out (participation). The agreement is, of course, the most important means of sight communication that will be used in the session.

When the copies have been distributed, he can ask if any members have seen it before, if so where and on what occasion and for what purposes; where members may consult a copy and so on. He can go on to ask members, without looking at the text, to say what they know about its contents, so that one by one the main headings can be written on the baord: wages, working hours, leave, etc. No doubt some of them may cheat at this point, but no matter - he has set the ball rolling. He can use the same technique in filling in the details of the different clauses. In this way, the entire document can be built up by a process of discussion and information-exchange in which much if not most of the oral presentation will be done by the members themselves, with the lecturer guiding the process and providing the important sight element by making full use of his blackboard and by drawing attention when convenient to the text of the printed agreement.

Where members have first-hand experience of certain clauses of the agreement, such as implementation provisions and grievance procedures, that experience will be invaluable to illustrate the lecture, quite apart from its use as a peg for discussion. Members who have been involved in the grievance procedure, for example, may be invited to explain the case: the grievance, the way it was handled and the outcome. The ensuing discussion is certain to be lively!

If separate sessions are to be held on grievance procedures, labour department conciliation arrangements, arbitration tribunals and other provisions of the agreement for settling differences, members with personal experience of cases might be asked to prepare their material beforehand, with all the relevant facts and figures, so that each in turn may take the place of the official lecturer in front of the class, while the latter steps to one side or physically changes place with the member concerned. Alternatively, he might act as a sort of amanuensis, doing the blackboard work if the speaker lacks confidence to do that himself. In so doing, he would incidentally be giving a useful demonstration of note-taking.

Where the participant's experience is to be exploited in this way, the lecturer must none the less have plenty of typical examples at his finger-tips, with which if necessary he can supplement, corroborate and amplify the material contributed by the members. He must be ready to comment on the substance of the participants' cases (not on the presentation, unless it is also a course for prospective lecturers) and to draw out the main points - always, of course, in consultation with the class as a whole. Above all, he must not allow any misconceptions to be perpetuated. Indeed, one of the benefits of this type of exercise is often that it enables the lecturer to clear up commonly held misunderstandings about the various procedures and about the substantive clauses of the agreement which have given rise to the incident.

A session of this sort, in which much of the experience is communicated by the participants, begins to merge with another popular teaching technique - the use of case histories and case studies - which is described a little later in this guide. At the present stage, the suggestion is simply that a lecturer may find he can draw on the participant's experience to illustrate his general exposition of a subject for the non-specialist or in the introductory stage of a longer course.

It need hardly be said that the mixture of sight, sound, discussion and practice at which the lecturer can aim will vary greatly with the subject. Where, for example, the subject is the union's own constitutional procedures, the participants may have a lot to contribute. Where it is a more concrete subject such as statistics, their eloquence will be more restrained.

Statistics, a different emphasis

There are really two basic things to be learned about the statistics of collective bargaining: why they are important (how to use them) and how to calculate them. Many good negotiators understand the first without being very clear about the second, though that is not a desirable state of affairs. Discussion and the participant's experience can be used to quite some extent in teaching the first; less so in the second. This weakness, however, can be offset by greater use of sight (endless use of the blackboard, statistical tables, etc.) and of the fourth factor, practice.

While there is much to be said for giving the participants a number of exercises to work out in their own time at the end of the lecture, practice should not be deferred until then. Problems should be set and solved continually during the session, with different participants invited by the lecturer to come forward and perform the calculation on the blackboard, while the remainder observe and, if necessary, dissent.

This is an occasion where it is often better not to call for volunteers, else only the brighter participants may come forward. On the other hand, the lecturer must be confident that the lesson (whatever it might be) has been generally understood; he will have no desire to humiliate the slower learners. The purpose, remember, is practice; that is, the practice of something that has already been learned. It is not the same as in teaching grievance procedure, for example, where one participant may have experience to contribute and another not, or the contents of the collective agreement, where one may have the information and the other not. We are now in the realm of _performance_. If a participant cannot perform a particular calculation, it is for the lecturer to explain the steps again until the method is finally grasped, privately if need be.

Striking a balance

At this point it might be as well to emphasise that the lecturer, in his desire to obtain participation, should not persist in trying to enlist the co-operation of the participants when it is clear that they have nothing to contribute. If he asks if any can give the dates of the collective agreement, for example, and it quickly becomes evident that nobody has the faintest idea, he should immediately provide the information himself and pass on to his next point. Similarly with more complex questions. If, on the other hand, the lecturer knows some of the participants have something to contribute but are held back by lack of confidence or by uncertainty as to the relevance of their information, he can throw out clues and in other ways ease them out of their reticence, until he is getting the level of response he desires.

There is also the opposite risk, that discussion will become so lively and protracted that the essential purpose of education - which is, after all, the transmission of knowledge - will be frustrated. The lecturer presumably knows more about the subject than anyone else present, hence his contribution must be decisive. If a subject is highly controversial, there is something to be said for the traditional practice of allotting a period for question and discussion at the end of the session, permitting only enough discussion in passing as is needed to heighten interest and bring out the points to be taken up later. The lecturer can write the points on the blackboard as they occur. It is a matter of striking the right balance between the lecturer's contribution and that of the participants in a co-operative quest for knowledge.

The lecturer knows what that knowledge is. At the end of the session, he must be satisfied that the participants have learned what he set out to teach. The participants have exactly the same interest.

Thorough preparation essential

In preparing a lecture, the essential thing is to note the knowledge that has to be communicated, stage by stage. The lecturer can then indicate techniques that might be employed at various points - ask questions, invite instances, promote discussion, use blackboard, distribute documents, etc. If he is lucky enough to have some more or less sophisticated technical aids, such as a tape-recording or a film strip, he must decide just at which point to introduce them and how to make best use of them. After he has given his lecture a few times, he will be able to manage with only the briefest basic notes - the main points to be covered. The assumption here is that film strips and tape-recordings will not take up the whole or the major part of the session. Their purpose in this instance is to illustrate a lecture.

Panel discussion

A development of the one-man lecture is the "brain's trust" or panel discussion in which two or more experts explore the subject by dealing with questions put to them by the participants, or cover the ground between them with the guidance of a tactful chairman. A panel of union officials responsible for different aspects of collective bargaining, for example, can be made up for this purpose. A disadvantage is the lack of member participation, except for the purpose of putting the questions; it is rather like a television discussion in that respect. On the other hand, it provides variety and the listeners feel they are benefitting from the experience of several experts, not only one. A discussion can always be arranged afterwards if time allows. It is often a good idea to introduce a panel session of this sort with a short film, film strip or tape-recording, and the use of the blackboard is not ruled out. If appropriate, panel members may make brief notes on the board occasionally, or the chairman may chalk up salient points as they arise. Documents, too, can of course be distributed and used in the same way as with the one-man lecture.

Again as with the one-man lecture, the chairman must prepare careful notes beforehand, if possible in consultation with the panel members, to make sure that when the session is over the intended knoweldge has in fact been communicated. A brief preparatory discussion between the panel members is always useful to decide what are the main points each will bring out, the sequence in which they will be invited to make their short introductory remarks before embarking on general discussion, to comment on the chairman's opening statement, on the film show or whatever has been used to start off the session. A good crisp ending is also important, with, if necessary, the main lessons summarised and made explicit. Just how this is to be contrived must also be agreed upon in advance. In our concern to make education entertaining, we must never forget that the priority is the education, not the entertainment.

IX. MORE TEACHING TECHNIQUES: CASE ANALYSES, ROLE-PLAYING

There is a slight difference between the case history and the case study, but it is largely a matter of emphasis. The case history is an actual case, dissected for the lessons it contains: the anatomy of collective bargaining, so to speak. The case study may be based on a real case, with which the participants are not too familiar, or it may be a concocted case designed to bring out certain points for discussion and possible answer. In other words, as far as the participants are concerned, it puts before them a hypothetical situation.

A case history should be as complete and as actual as possible. It will require a basic paper describing the case, supported by all the relevant documents, statistics, extracts from minutes of meetings, copies of principal statements made by the negotiating parties and so on. Copies of all this material can be distributed to the participants. If, in addition, there are tape-recordings of any part of the process, these can be played to the class.

There are unlikely to be films available as a general rule (unless there were public hearings or television interviews) but if it is thought worth doing, and there is plenty of time, parts of the proceedings could be re-enacted, with members of the union playing the various roles. If this were attempted, however, it would have to be a perfectly truthful reconstruction, with no caricaturing of the employers or government officials. There would be no scope for improvisation, as in the quite different technique of "role-playing", discussed later. It would be more akin to a play-reading than a role-playing.

When the history has been presented in as much detail and absorbed as thoroughly as time permits, the intended lessons can be drawn from it. The aim may be simply to illustrate the collective bargaining process, in which event the lecturer or discussion leader will identify the main elements, in consultation with the class, employing some of the lecturing techniques already described. Or it may go further than that: it may be to study the strengths and weaknesses of the union's case, of the manner in which it was pressed and of the tactics employed. In that event, the class, as before, might be divided into groups, each with a rapporteur, to discuss the matter in separate meetings and to come together again at a later stage to compare their conclusions. If this discussion group technique is used, the course leader may, if he thinks it desirable, provide a list of points to guide the discussions. What those points should be, however, must itself be briefly discussed and agreed upon before the groups separate.

Case histories are usually by their nature fairly complex, except where they deal with the simplest of workshop grievances, in which event they are of interest more as illustrations than for purposes of analysis. The material need not be new to the participants; there is indeed sometimes something to be said for analysing cases with which they have some rough acquaintance. The case study also may be quite complex, or it may contain only a few simple elements, creating a problem which may not, however, be so easy to solve, and the participants would normally have no previous knowledge of the details. An example of a fairly complex case is given in Annex 2, which describes the situation in a hypothetical footwear factory. Whether the case is relatively simple or complex, the group's assignment is to propose what it considers the best solution to the problem or problems presented.

The case study

It has already been observed that the case study and to a lesser degree the case history are practical exercises, that is tests of knowledge and skill, as distinct from other discussion group techniques already mentioned, the essential purpose of which was to communicate or to consolidate knowledge, including knowledge gleaned from experience. In preparing material for a case study, therefore, course instructors will be thinking all the time of the exercise or exercises which may be based on it and may add a list of these at the end of the case description, as is done in Annex 2. Where the case is a relatively simple one, the process can be reversed: the exercise decided first and a case concocted for the purpose.

Where the law is or might be involved, for example, that would be the obvious method. The case would be carefully constructed to lead to such exercises as (a) indicate what laws and regulations, if any, have been broken in this case; (b) state the legal aspects of this case; (c) prepare a statement for submission during collective bargaining or before an arbitration tribunal, covering the legal aspects of this case. It will be noted that even these straightforward exercises progress in complexity, the third one requiring judgement and skill in exposition as well as knowledge of the law. Remember in this connection that "the law" includes the existing collective agreement if enforceable in the courts.

If statistics are featured in the case study, it must be remembered that the purpose of the study is to bring out the conclusions to be derived from them and also, possibly, to propose ways in which the statistical arguments might be developed and advanced in the bargaining process. Also, is the statistical information adequate? The assumption at this stage must be that the underlying mathematics have been firmly grasped. Annex 2 suggests a simple statistical case study. Be it noted, by the way, that company accounts are a collection of statistics, and make excellent case study material.

Role-playing

The case study gets very close at times to the last major technique we shall discuss in this guide, that of role-playing. A participant who has been required to prepare and then read out a dissertation on the legal or statistical aspects of a case, for example, has briefly impersonated the union official who would perform that task in real life. That performance, however, has been a solo effort, written and quite possibly rehearsed in advance. Role-playing normally involves more characters, calls for greater improvisation and generally has a beginning, a middle and an end.

If participants were required to prepare a press statement, for example, on the basis of given information (a case study) that

would not by itself constitute role-playing unless the exercise
continued with a simulated press conference in which various people
played the roles of the media representatives. In that example, a
role-play with only two characters would just be possible, one
performing the part of the union leader, the other that of a
newspaper man who was interviewing him. Similarly, one can envisage
a role-play in which a single union representative confronted a
single employer or labour department representative. Generally,
however, the situation played out in the role-play will be more
complex.

The role-play situation must be carefully worked out in
advance, in much the same way as a case study. Many case studies,
in fact, lend themselves very readily to role-playing exercises; for
example, the hypothetical footwear factory case described in Annex
2. If great care has not been taken when preparing the background,
participants will be tempted to invent "facts" to support their case
during the play, or the action itself may falter or stall altogether
because information essential for the development of the situation
is unknown.

If either side introduces unprepared "facts", the other side
should of course ask for an adjournment, during which all concerned
in the role-play can come to an understanding on what the "facts"
should be before the exercise is resumed, but this expedient is
clearly not very satisfactory in cases where in real life the
information in question would be freely available. This,
incidentally, is one of the reasons why there is much to be said for
basing case studies and role-playing exercises on real cases
wherever possible, since it is extremely difficult, not to say
laborious, to identify every fact that might be relevant to a
hypothetical situation, except the most simple. Needless to say,
situations should still be selected of which the participants
themselves have little or no previous knowledge.[1]

Aim is not entertainment

Wherever possible, participants in role-playing exercises
should not be called upon to perform parts they will not normally be
required to fill in real life. This does not mean that a union
member must never be expected to impersonate a high-ranking union
officer, because some day he may become such a person himself. The
roles of employers, managers, labour department officials and such
characters, however, should be played by instructors, union
officials and others who in real life have dealt with such persons
and know what they are really like. Moreover, they must try
sincerely to reproduce these characters accurately, without
distortion or even humour. The temptation to gag the boss's
representatives, above all, must be resisted. It can be very funny,
but it is not education.

In a certain role-playing session in a developing country in
which a simulated meeting of a works council was arranged, the
question at issue was the interpretation of the collective agreement
in two instances, one concerning overtime, the other dismissal. The
----

[1] In a guide of this sort, for obvious reasons, we have to stick
to hypothetical examples.

company had a number of branches, in some of which works councils had functioned quite effectively for a relatively long time, but this works council was quite new. Permission had been granted to hold the simulated meeting on company premises in the room where the council would normally meet.

The parts of the workers' representatives were played by the actual workers recently elected to the works council, who were quite new to the task. The management representatives were played by students from the local university whose studies included labour law and to some extent industrial relations. It was thought that they, too, might benefit from the exercise. A document describing the two cases - a case study - had previously been distributed and the two sides had held separate meetings to discuss it and decide tactics.

On the whole, all concerned played their parts well, though two of the students with a gift for farce produced hilarious caricatures of peppery old gentlemen, which they apparently believed to be portraits of typical management representatives. This was good fun for the onlookers, but it was quite clearly not appreciated by the workers' representatives, who had come to learn something about how to discharge their new responsibilities and expected, very properly that the ocasion would be taken seriously. This was a useful illustration of the importance of choosing the players who are to impersonate "the other side" from the ranks of those who have some first-hand experience of the process, whichever side they may be on in real life.

After the role-play, one of the company's junior personnel officers who had agreed to assist, a young woman, explained that the two cases had in fact occurred at other branches and that the argument in the actual hearings had developed on essentially the same lines as in the role-play, except that the workers' representatives in the simulated hearing had taken longer to latch on to the vital points.

The role-play ended, as pre-arranged, with the management offering to give the cases further consideration. This was how it had happened in real life, and the young personnel officer was able to report to the group that in the event the management had in fact felt obliged to concede the unions' claims on behalf of its aggrieved members. The visible satisfaction of the workers' role-play representatives on hearing this news was good to behold. All agreed afterwards that the exercise had been the best possible way of familiarising them with the procedure and in giving them confidence to perform their new duties.

Unlimited possibilities

A role-playing exercise need not, of course, be restricted to a single scene. If a works council meeting on the lines of the above example were included in a broader exercise, for example, any of the following scenes could be depicted if thought helpful: the incidents that gave rise to the hearing; the members reporting to the shop-steward or branch official, who questions them shrewdly to make sure he has received all the relevant information; the union representative or representatives taking up the case with management; the report-back to the branch or union works committee, which resolves that the case be placed on the agenda of the next

meeting of the works council; the meeting of the council, followed
perhaps by further report-back meetings, arbitration proceedings and
even a similated law case.

It is for programme planners to decide how much a role-play
can accomplish in the available time. Generally, the action will be
restricted to a few fairly straightforward situations. At the end
of long residential courses, however, very ambitious role-playing
exercises have been devised lasting several sessions, in which
everything the participants have learned about collective bargaining
has been introduced - preparing the claim, the union's democratic
procedures, committee meetings, press conferences, the use (if
relevant) of labour department consultations and so on. Above all,
the bargaining sessions with the employers can be taken through
several different phases when there is adequate time. Any
participants who have specialised in particular aspects of the
process, such as the basic economics and statistics, can play their
appropriate roles as advisers to the negotiating team.

Because collective bargaining, whatever its precise form, is
essentially a process of peaceful confrontation and reconciliation,
role-playing is the practical exercise which comes closest to
reality, and for many participants it is the only way in which they
can learn by personal experience. Its potential in teaching
collective bargaining should therefore be fully exploited.

To obtain the maximum benefit, there should always be a frank
discussion of the lessons illustrated by the exercise after each
role-playing session - a post-mortem. This will be not only
valuable in itself but will involve members who have not taken part
in the role-play as such. If role-playing is to be used
extensively, however, care must be taken that all members take part
at some time or another. Even the same scene can be done more than
once with different players before the remainder of the class.

Different techniques combined

It will be observed that now we have begun to combine
different techniques; role-playing with discussion, for example.
One could go further. The post-mortem could also be group
discussion, and since the role-play will have depicted aspects of a
particular case, the technique of the case history and the case
study have also been introduced at the discussion stage. The entire
procedure might have been introduced by a lecture and rounded off by
comments from a panel of experts. Written exercises might have been
required at certain points.

The fact that in this guide it has been found convenient to
describe various techniques separately does not mean that they are
necessarily to be separated in practice, or even that one technique
can always be distinguished clearly from another when in use. What
is important is that programme planners and their colleagues should
devise an effective mixture of techniques for teaching the subject
to the intended membership group. Mixing the techniques is itself
a technique, a technique for retaining interest. If overdone, role-
playing itself can become as boring and as irritating as the old-
fashioned one-man lecture, and without, in all probability,
conveying as much information.

Above all, the techniques cannot be divorced from the persons available to employ them and the teaching material at their disposal. This consideration is of special importance in workers' education, many of whose practitioners will not be full-time professionals and for which teaching material often has to be drawn from the union's own files. If you have a brilliant lecturer, use him; give him his head, as the saying goes! If you have volunteers whose union experience makes them experts in their field, whose heads so to speak are union files full of valuable documents, put them on a panel. If you have a recent case of outstanding value for the lessons to be drawn from it, set up a case analysis session followed by group discussion. Ask yourself all the time: who have we got, what have we got, to teach this item?

Recapitulation: the three planning stages

The three essential stages in planning a collective bargaining course, as in all workers' education programmes are:

(1)   define clearly the type of member to be taught;

(2)   draw up a detailed syllabus tailor-made to fit him, which later, if need be, can be rendered in a more condensed form;

(3)   go through the syllabus item by item, noting the techniques or combination of techniques most likely to be effective in teaching them, always bearing in mind the personnel and the material likely to be available and always applying to the greatest extent practicable the SSDP formula: sound, sight, discussion, practice.

The first two phases should be carried out in consultation with the members concerned; the second, if at all possible, with all the persons who at one time or another may be conducting the course. At these early stages, as at all later stages, the key word is - participation.

————————

ANNEX 1

Example of a basic statistical exercise

At the time, two years previously, when the current agreement came into effect, the statistics given in column A applied. Column B indicates the latest position.

	A	B
Cost-of-living index	148	174
Company's profits before tax	203 000	234 000
Taxes paid	42 000	51 000
Dividend distributed (after tax)	98 000	119 000
Minimum monthly wage	80/00	80/00
Number on minimum	880	1 010
Average pay of other employees	102/20	116/40
Number of such employees	140	230
Average monthly earnings in the same economic sector	98/00	102/50
Average all sectors	112/10	134/00

For the purpose of the exercise assume (a) that working hours are not an issue, (b) that overtime is not normally worked, (c) that average monthly earnings cover all workers up to the level of shop foreman or the equivalent, and (d) that the only taxes for which the company is liable is a 30 per cent tax on distributed profits.

Exercise: The union is negotiating a new monthly minimum wage. What should it claim? What is the least it should be willing to accept? List the statistics which (a) strengthen its case, (b) weaken its case. Suggest arguments which might be advanced to counter the latter. Do not invent additional facts, but assume that the various trends revealed by the statistics - e.g. cost of living, national wage trends - are expected to continue for the duration of the new agreement, i.e. two years.

Note to instructor: One of the first steps will be to render appropriate statistics into percentages, to enable direct comparisons to be made. For example, the cost of living has increased 17.6 per cent, profits 15.3 per cent, average earnings in the country as a whole 19.5 per cent, dividends 21.4 per cent, etc. Total wage bill can be worked out, profit per worker, cost of proposed increases, etc., including (if proposed) any cost-of-living increments to be incorporated in the union's claim. Group discussion, role-playing, etc., can be developed out of exercises of this sort.

ANNEX 2.A

A simulation exercise in collective bargaining

The Quality Footwear case

General information

The Quality Footwear shoe manufacturing plant has been in
operation in the capital city for more than ten years. The plant is
one of two similar establishments, operating under different names,
owned by Progress Company Ltd., an indigenous company financed
mainly through private investments and to a smaller extent with the
help of a 20-year interest-free loan from the National Development
Corporation. The other factory is located in another part of the
country and is operating under separate directorship. In addition
to these two plants the company also owns other industrial
undertakings.

The operation of the factory is mainly arranged by way of
production lines, with the tannery sector supplying the lines with
material. In such a system the product, in this case the shoe,
gradually passes through a number of assembly stations. At each
station a number of predetermined operations are performed, each
adding one or several details to the shoe, which in the process
gradually moves closer to its final shape. It leaves the last
station ready to wear and is then passed on to the store awaiting
distribution to the shops. Cutting the leather in set patterns is
made at separate stations, in the first stage of the operation,
after which the elements together with other material needed in the
process are delivered at the different stations. Depending on the
complexity of the operation the number of workers and machines at
each station is calculated so as to permit an even flow of partially
finished products through the line.

The method is a rational way of production but also one that
is highly vulnerable to interruptions, as experience has already
shown. If for some reason the work at one station is stopped, the
next station will soon run out of material, while at the same time
partly finished shoes are piling up at the place of the stoppage.

After a rather difficult introduction period of more than five
years during which the plant experienced considerable problems in
establishing itself on the market, the demand on the plant's
products started to increase and in recent years it has been run at
full capacity.

A matter of deep concern to the management, which has been the
subject of numerous discussions between the two managerial
assistants and the shop-stewards, is the unsatisfactory productivity
with irregular output and deficiencies in quality. Comparison with
imported shoes at the same price levels have proved that, in many
cases, the plant's products are not of the same quality as imported
shoes. Substandards were discovered both in the leather itself and
in the way the parts are joined together along the production line.

The most important reasons for the poor workmanship are
difficulties in finding and retaining skilled workers. The problem

is most prominent in the tanning sector but can be found also along the production line. Attempts to solve the problem with the help of closer supervision have not been very successful. Good training for tanning work can only be found abroad and is thus very costly.

The management maintains, although shop-stewards mostly disagree with this view, that the main reason for irregular and low output is a high degree of absenteeism which on several occasions has severely affected the smooth running of the production line - even to the extent of bringing it to a complete stand-still for hours. Solving the problem by transferring available workers over to empty or undermanned stations has only given limited improvement. Transferred workers are naturally less familiar with the new tasks and thus less effective. It appears that some workers, resisting transfer, also have resorted to low performance.

The trade union organisation representing the workers at the plant is the General Workers' Union (GWU). A local branch union has been established at the plant, with its own committee and with four elected shop-stewards, one each for the tannery, production line, the store and the office.

After an initial phase of poor industrial relations at the plant when the management refused to recognise the union and it, in turn, countered with several short strikes, a working relationship was finally established with the help of a senior labour officer. Grievances occur, but with no more than normal frequency, and it is normally possible to settle the differences within the plant without having to resort to the government conciliation machinery.

All workers are on monthly wages. Promotion to higher grade in the same unit is routinely made after the worker has completed stipulated time in the grade, normally two years. Semi-skilled labourers having acquired sufficient experience are promoted to craftsmen's grade to fill vacancies. For a craftsman in the tannery sector to be promoted to technicians' grade a special training course is required. New workers already possessing the required experience may be placed in the grade according to skill after an examination undertaken by either of the two sectoral assistant managers. Technicians, assisted by craftsmen, are responsible for processing the hides in the tanning sector. Other craftsmen operate the production line. Labourers perform the work of moving material around in both sectors as well as other work of a general character in the whole plant.

The workforce, below the level of junior management, stands at 412 persons, as follows:

Sector	Title of post	Number	Wages
Tannery	Foreman	1	1 300
	Technician Grade I	8	1 200
	Technician Grade II	12	1 040
	Craftsman Grade I	14	755
	Craftsman Grade II	20	715
	Labourer, semi-skilled	8	600
	Labourer, unskilled	25	560
Production line	Foreman	2	1 350
	Assistant foreman	4	1 100
	Headman	4	900
	Craftsman, Grade I	45	755
	Craftsman, Grade II	84	715
	Labourer, semi-skilled	17	600
	Labourer, unskilled	50	560
Office	Clerk, Grade I	12	1 250
	" " II	18	1 000
	" " III	28	720
	" " IV	23	560
	Messenger	5	375
Store	Storekeeper	1	1 200
	Assistant storekeeper	3	900
	Store attendant	21	560
Transport	Driver	7	680

All workers are members of the union. The collective agreement regulates the pay at all grades. None the less, the foremen and technicians are looked upon by the other workers as being more closely linked with the management.

About 30 per cent of the total workforce are women. The same pay scales are used for women as for men. The majority of the women are found in the unskilled labourers' and store attentants' group, with only a few having reached the craftsmen's grades. Turnover is considerably higher among women than among men and this seems to have prevented the women from acquiring sufficient experience for promotion to craftsmen's category.

Besides regulating the wages, the collective agreement also provides for a number of fringe benefits. The most important of these are the following:

- paid annual leave of 15 to 30 days depending on length of service, with maximum requiring 15 years' service;

- sick leave with pay, maximum 10 days a year;

- free medical service including prescribed medicine;

- maternity leave with full pay for one month and half pay for an additional month of each pregnancy;

- retirement gratuity of one month's pay for each year in service for each worker with more than five years' service.

The agreement also recognises the GWU as the sole bargaining union at the plant, regulates grievance procedures and how the check-off will be operated.

The present collective agreement is due to expire shortly and the union has already notified the management in writing of its intention to have the terms of the agreement renegotiated. The notice did not provide any details about the union's claims apart from stating that wage increases will have to be substantial.

Specific information concerning the management

The Board of the Progress Company Ltd. meets normally only twice a year. The purpose of the meetings is normally to take decisions on policy matters and issues of principal and major importance such as investments, business results and projections, the general position of individual undertakings under its ownership, occasionally to appoint a plant manager, etc. The current affairs of both mother company and subsidiaries are left for the Chairman of the Board to handle. He, in turn, prefers to allow each manager the greatest possible freedom of operation, being convinced that this is the best way of operating a big company. Only in connection with very important issues and after having been consulted by the manager does he involve himself directly in the daily activities of a plant.

Contacts between the two shoe plant managers are rare and mostly confined to occasional discussions about prices and availability of raw material, import problems and duties, etc. There is no co-ordination in respect of wages, sales prices, production and related matters.

The Quality Footwear plant has for the last few years been operating at a profit, but has not yet been in a position to compensate shareholders for low dividends during the early years. Even though the manager prefers to demonstrate a position of full confidence in the future, he is inwardly fully aware of the fact that without the 30 per cent import duty, to which all imported footwear is subjected, it would be extremely difficult to compete with the prices of imported shoes.

Concern in this respect has been increased by recent rumours that the Government is contemplating discontinuing import duties on shoes - or at least reducing the tariffs considerably. A hint in the same direction was a recent editorial in one of the influential daily newspapers in which the wisdom and fairness of maintaining heavy import duties on such essential commodities as shoes, and in particular the cheaper brands used by workers, was questioned. The prospect of having eventually to compete on an unprotected market is not a happy one. He feels strongly that it will be necessary to find ways by which the increased competition can be met and that these measures need to be implemented as soon as possible. The fact that this has to be accomplished with productivity at an unsatisfactory level does not make the task easy.

Having discussed the issue repeatedly with his two assistants he has arrived at the conclusion that only with the help of an incentive wage system (sometimes called payment-by-result) will it be possible to increase the productivity sufficiently to overcome

existing problems and meet the expected ones. He is well aware that
the union is strongly opposed to any kind of incentive schemes but
as things stand he can see no way around the problem. Also, the
seriousness of the situation should be enough to convince the union
that some kind of flexibility on this matter is necessary in order
to avoid a situation which can easily develop into a real threat to
the jobs of its members. Also, the argument that a well working
incentive scheme, besides improving productivity, will give workers
a chance to increase their pay in accordance with their own efforts,
should, he feels, certainly bear considerable weight in discussions
directly with workers.

The exact structure of the scheme to be used has not yet been
determined. He would prefer individual piece rates as most
stimulative for each worker, but realises that with a production
line system in use individual rates would be very difficult to
apply. Some kind of a bonus system tied to the output of the whole
sector and shared between all the workers in the sector, would be
more appropriate. However, this question will have to wait until
the talks with the union are under way.

As he sees it, the problem related to quality deficiences will
have to be dealt with in two different ways. One will be to
strengthen quality control before the shoes are passed on to the
store. Combined with a regulation that failure to meet minimum
quality standards will reduce the bonus to which the sector may be
entitled, to a corresponding degree, he hopes this may be enough to
restore the previous quality level.

He feels, however, that not even this will be enough to solve
the problem in the tannery sector. To keep the best trained
technicians from leaving the plant direct wage increases for this
group are evidently needed. The manager is therefore prepared to
add two more grades to the existing scale for this group. This will
give the workers with long service an immediate increase and provide
others with something to look forward to. As a consequence, also,
the foremen too will have to be upgraded.

In the forthcoming negotiations the manager is determined to
stall all discussions about wage increases in favour of an all-out
discussion about present and foreseen problems and the need to find
ways to strengthen the position of the plant. The proposal for a
new wage system will then be introduced and a presentation of
possible incentive schemes follow. He envisages that there will be
a need for many more meetings before all these matters can be
settled. Only when a solution to these important matters seems to
be near will an offer of a nominal general wage increase, merely as
additional inducement, be made, followed by an explanation of the
intended changes in technicians' scales.

Specific information about the union and its position

The General Workers' Union (GWU) would, with both recognition
and check-off agreements in operation, appear to have a strong hold
on the organisation of the workers at the plant. But the General
Secretary of the National Union can remember the struggle only a few
years ago when the Factory and Industrial Workers' Union (FWU),
which organises the workers at the other shoe plant, tried to win

his members into its fold. It took a long time to win that fight and the FWU would certainly be quick to grab the first opportunity, for instance widespread discontent among the workers, to reopen the issue.

The Secretary is also well aware that not everything is as it should be at the plant. The Branch Secretary has informed him about growing irritation among the members as a result of the workers constantly being shifted around in the plant, never getting a chance to settle properly in any place. On top of that the management has started complaining increasingly about high absenteeism and low productivity and to threaten to introduce some kind of piece-rate wage system. This has added to the normal agitation about inflation and low wages normally to be expected in the present situation.

The GS is determined to get tough with the management on all these issues. He believes the management should be made to realise its responsibility to organise production in such a way that the workers should not constantly be harassed in their work. As far as piece-rate systems are concerned the General Secretary holds strongly that these are only devices for further exploitation of the workers, and will have to be stopped at all costs. In that he has succeeded before and is not overly concerned now.

Inflation is another issue that will have to receive priority in any negotiations at present. According to the union's calculations price increases for the last two years, e.g. since the agreement was signed, now exceed 15 per cent, and have seriously eroded the value of the gains made in the agreement. It may well be that prices on essential commodities like food and clothing have risen even more than the average. The union expects that this development will continue, if not get worse, over the year to come. To the best of the union's estimates the plant must have been doing quite well during the last few years, running at full capacity as it has. It is only fair that the workers get a share of the profit, and he feels strongly that a claim for a wage increase of 35 per cent is fully motivated.

When he attended the branch union general meeting the members approved this stand with a standing ovation. He will present the claim orally in the bargaining session to which he will be accompanied by the secretary, the president and the four shop-stewards of the branch union.

About the exercise and its use

The general information provided about the Quality Footwear undertaking, on which the exercise is based, its operations, internal structure, business situation, etc., is rather detailed, more so perhaps than in many a real collective bargaining situation. The reason for this has been a wish to provide a sufficiently detailed picture to enable course participants to see and understand as much as possible, not only of the collective bargaining procedure as demonstrated, but also something about the complicated, not to say intricate, background picture normally prevailing in each collective bargaining activity where wages and conditions of work are at issue. To be successful in his task any collective bargaining practitioner will need to know as much as possible about this background in order to be in the best position to judge proposals from and reactions of the other side and to be able to estimate whether a particular position taken by the other side is based on actual financial or other facts or if it should merely be regarded as a temporary defence line from which a retreat may be made if the right arguments are produced. The background information will also be most useful when it comes to formulating alternative proposals and compromises which, although intended to carry maximum benefit for the union members, still also will have to be acceptable to the other side.

An additional reason for the multiplicity of information is the hope that this will contribute to the emergence of additional issues during the process. The most prominent issue, as far as workers are concerned, is of course the demand for wage increases. But we have also been informed that the management has its own intentions and is determined to bring up the issue of payment by result. This may, in turn, lead to discussion about various forms of incentive pay schemes and their pros and cons in relation to productivity, absenteeism, pay, working conditions, etc. Other issues that members of the teams may wish to bring up include the position of female workers, the establishment of a proper training scheme, etc.

In fact the range of subjects, directly or indirectly related to the position of the workers in the factory, is very wide and most of them will need to be discussed and clarified and their importance to be judged.

Depending on the use the instructor intends to make of the exercise the background information should be distributed with selectivity so as to accomplish the greatest possible impact of the case. More about this later. The instructor may also wish to include more information in order to increase its relevance to a particular situation. Such adaptations may be very useful, but great care should be taken not to include "facts" that may tend to distort the exercise by making it contraditory or unbalanced.

Wages have been listed without stating any specific currency thus permitting the use of the currency in the country where the exercise is being used. Some adjustment of the scales may be necessary in order to reflect more accurately the situation in a particular country.

The exercise may be used in different ways to suit a particular training situation. Three ways will be described here in detail. In the annexes below is given a step-by-step instruction in how to conduct the exercise.

Alternative one concentrates on role-playing. The purpose of this alternative is, in particular, to demonstrate to an uninformed audience what collective bargaining is and how it may be conducted and develop.

Alternative two goes deeper, aiming at a practical involvement of all participants who, divided into small bargaining teams, attempt to undertake the collective bargaining required to settle the differences between management and workers/union at the Quality Footwear Company.

Alternative three, finally, consists of a number of shorter exercises that may be held if time does not permit of extensive role-playing sessions.

ANNEX 2.B

Alternative one and Alternative two

1. Time allocation, need for rooms and helpers

In order to permit all the various points and issues emerging from the exercise to be sufficiently projected and to provide enough time for a thorough discussion of what took place at least two full days should be set aside for this alternative.

Normally the exercise will call for at least two small rooms in addition to the main classrooms in which the course is being held. All three rooms should be fitted with chalk boards or similar teaching aids.

The instructor will need the assistance of two helpers to guide and assist the teams in their work and to function as liaison men between the instructor and the teams. The assistants should preferably have at least some experience of collective bargaining.

2. Introduction

The instructor begins with a careful explanation of the exercise, its purpose, the methods to be used and what will be expected both of the team members and other participants in the course. After this participants are given the first part of the details of the exercise (general information) and time to study it.

3. Selection of teams

The exercise calls for two negotiating teams, one representing the union, the other the management. The teams should normally not contain more than four to six persons. The selection of the union team normally offers no problem. At least one person with some experience of collective bargaining should be included if there are participants with such experience.

Finding suitable members for the management team is often a little more difficult. It should be borne in mind that a managent team should be depicted as realistically as possible, without attempts at ridiculing or overdramatising. It has sometimes been found that worker participants have difficulties in identifying themselves in these roles and to act them with realism. Sometimes an outsider, perhaps a labour officer or a personnel officer, can be recruited to assist as a member of the management team. If no other solution can be found and a management team consisting entirely of workers is found unsatisfactory, the instructor will have to assume the role of leader of the management team.

4. Team preparation

The two teams withdraw to two separate rooms, each with the assistance of a helper. For their deliberations the management team will receive the specific information concerning the management while the union team receives the specific information about the union and its position. Normally half an hour should be enough for each team to read the information and to discuss its position for the ensuing bargaining session.

In the meantime the remaining participants, forming the audience, continue to discuss and digest the general information.

Having completed their preparations the teams are called to present their claims to the audience, one team at a time, and to give some brief indication of the tactics each intends to use in the discussions.

The purpose of this session is to let the audience know the initial position of each team, the better to follow the development of arguments and compromises in the ensuing discussions.

5.   Bargaining starts

After these preparations the two teams meet for the first bargaining session, also in front of the audience, to submit their claims and to receive those of the other team. In this first session it will normally not be possible to proceed further than to present claims, to clarify by means of questions and answers the exact meaning of each claim and, possibly, to outline briefly the argumentation in support of these.

When this has been done an adjournment for internal consultation should be proposed and accepted. Both teams then withdraw for separate discussion about the situation as it looks at this stage. During these considerations a team may, or may not, find fit to adjust its previous stand in the light of what has been said by the opposite side.

Meanwhile the audience discusses what has just taken place and receives clarification by the instructor, if need be, so as to be absolutely clear about the claims and counterclaims. For this purpose it will be useful if the helpers have already listed the claims of each team for the instructor's use.

6.   Second bargaining session

The teams reappear in front of the audience to present their actual position and to start the real bargaining. This may include specific counterproposals to claims having been received during the previous session from the opposite team. In any case this session will be characterised by an exhaustive discussion of each position in which all arguments in favour of both teams' claims are developed. When the instructor feels that the positions have been sufficiently clarified and that little new is coming up in the discussion he arranges for a new adjournment.

The instructor must follow the discussion very closely and make sure that the debate is not going round in circles with the same arguments being advanced and refuted again and again. The helpers will have made notes of all points the teams have decided to bring up during their closed sessions, to make sure that these are in fact included in the discussion. For this purpose it may be necessary occasionally to make discreet interventions with the team leader.

During the second adjournment each team will adjust its position further to claims made by the opposite side if it feels it can reasonably do so and at the same time review its own claims to see what modifications might be possible in order to facilitate as far as possible the reaching of an agreement.

Part of these deliberations may take place in front of the audience, each team appearing separately, to provide a picture of how the discussions are progressing.

It will again be the responsibility of the helpers to advise the teams in finding possibilities of compromise, if these exist, and how far such compromises might go.

7.   Third bargaining session

This is the last bargaining session and a conclusion will have to be reached, either a settlement or a breakdown.

What form a possible settlement should take or, in the opposite case, what obstacles may lead to a breakdown, obviously cannot be foreseen in these notes. The outcome will depend on the people involved, on their experience and on other factors mostly of a local character.

The instructor should endeavour to encourage a degree of flexibility and help through the helpers the development of a give-and-take approach without which few collective agreements are concluded.

8.   Concluding discussion

The purpose of the final discussion is to undertake a thorough analysis of the entire exercise. All participants, those who served on the teams as well as in the audience, will be helped to see and understand more of the whole exercise and thereby more of the complex concept of collective bargaining.

The discussion may usefully start with a further role-play in which each team reports back on the negotiations and the outcome. The union team might do so to a simulated branch union meeting and the management team to the chairman of the board. Each report is made in the absence of the other team and the audience observes the way in which it is presented, in particular as to accuracy. Is the reporting done in such a way that the audience clearly understands what it includes? Are the various aspects of the process adequately emphasised? How are the compromises explained? The first phase of the concluding discussion may thus form an evaluation of one very important aspect to any collective bargaining session - the report back.

The second phase of the concluding discussion will then focus on the negotiating process as such, how successfully did the audience find the performance, what kind of mistakes were made, which important points did either of the teams overlook in the argumentation with the other team, and other points similar in character.

Finally, is the agreement a good one, or at least the best possible? Alternatively, was the breakdown the only possible conclusion in the given situation? Would not some further compromises have been acceptable?

Note in particular that if the exercise has led to a breakdown it is most important to anlayse the situation. What will now be the situation for the workers concerned? Are there any other ways in resolving the situation? Conciliation? Arbitration? Industrial court? Strike?

Since the situation with regard to labour legislation particularly concerning the settlement of industrial disputes, varies considerably from country to country, it is not possible to provide any guidelines in that respect here. If the instructor is not familiar with the situation in the country in which the exercise is being performed it will be necessary to engage local expertise to provide the necessary information for this purpose.

1. Purpose, selection of participants

The purpose of this exercise, which is based on the same case as alternative one, is to demonstrate to a group of trade unionists, through active involvement in a simulated collective bargaining exercise, the process of collective bargaining and the role of a collective bargainer. In the process a brief training for the work of a trade union collective bargaining representative will be provided.

The exercise is primarily designed for local trade union leaders with bargaining responsibilities or other unionists in similar position who have little or no previous training for their tasks.

2. Time requirements

The technique used, while normally quite educative in character, is rather time-consuming. The minimum period required for a successful completion of the exercise would be about one full week. For maximum benefit to participants, permitting all the training aspects to be fully utilised, up to ten working days may be regarded as more useful.

3. Meeting rooms and other facilities required

In addition to the main meeting room used for plenary sessions of the course, each team will need a place where they can meet regularly for separate sessions to undertake preparatory work, discuss problems, formulate claims, etc.

All rooms should preferably be equipped with a chalk board or some other arrangement for writing on. Access to typewriters and even calculating machines will greatly facilitate the work of the teams and ease the task for the instructor.

Easy access to information regarding working conditions, statistics on wages, prices, etc., as well as legislation concerning other issues within the labour field, will make the work of the group easier and more realistic and thus contribute to its usefulness. These aspects should be included when the venue of a course is being considered.

4. Staffing

The instructor, who in addition to being in charge of the whole exercise also normally will have to assume the role of management bargainer, shall need the assistance of a number of helpers for his work. The task of one of those is, among other things, to keep record of all claims received from and proposals made to the teams. He shall also have to assist the instructor to keep record of all proposals and compromises made during the negotiations. The primary task of the two additional helpers will be to assist the teams in their work.

5. Introduction of the exercise

The instructor begins with a thorough introduction explaining the purpose of the exercise, how participants are to be involved in the work and generally how the exercise is planned to be conducted.

After this participants are given the general information about the Quality Footwear company case to study carefully and to retain for future consultation. Since the case forms the base from which all teams will operate it is important that the information is clearly understood and comprehended. A brief session for questions and clarifications may thus be useful for the elimination of any remaining misunderstanding.

Once the instructor is convinced that this part of the information is clear to everybody the information sheet containing specific information about the union and its position is to be distributed. Again a short session for questions and clarifications may be necessary. (The information concerning position of the management shall not be distributed at this stage.)

When the instructor is satisfied that all participants are familiar with the information they have received he proceeds to explain the methods to be used in the exercise - that the group will be divided into a number of small teams each of which shall assume the role of a union negotiation committee and who will separately be charged with the responsibility of negotiating a new collective agreement with the management of the Quality Footwear company.

The whole week shall be based on the information they have just received regarding this fictitious undertaking as well as of the trade union operating at the company, a branch of the General Workers' Union, which they will now be representing. The work of the teams will begin with the preparation and submission of claims, continue through repeated discussions with the management representative - to be played by the instructor - gathering of any supporting data that may be available for the purpose of supporting their own claims and/or providing information relating to management's proposal. The exercise will be completed when a new agreement has been signed, or in the unfortunate event that no agreement can be reached, when a deadlock has occurred.

It should be stressed that even though the information about the position of the QF company, such as financial position, number of workers, wages, etc., shall be taken to reflect actual facts from which no deviation can be made, the teams are at liberty to come up with any claim on behalf of the workers they may feel motivated - in the same way as they might do in a real bargaining situation. Such claims may concern wages, wage structure, wage systems, working conditions, fringe benefits, etc., but may as well extend into other areas such as, for instance, workers' participation or practically every aspect of working conditions or management/labour relations within the company.

6. Selection of teams

The composition of the bargaining teams requires considerable attention and should be undertaken with a view to creating teams that are as equal in strength, experience and competence as possible. The selection process may best be undertaken by the instructor assisted by his helpers before the exercise starts on the basis of information about participants contained in application forms or gained during earlier stages of the course. The aim should be to mix participants from different unions and branches and with various degrees of experience in each team. In case of participants with previous experience in collective bargaining these should also, as far as possible, be distributed among the teams for the purpose of utilising their experience in the best possible way.

Experience has shown that group work of this kind is normally most effectively performed in small groups containing from five to eight persons each. This arrangement permits all or most of the participants to get really involved in the work in a way that the less experienced or shy individuals would not be able to in a large group. Depending on the total number of participants some adjustment to this rule may have to be made in order to keep the number of teams within the limits of what the instructor (management bargainer) will be able to handle effectively. Normally an experienced instructor, assisted by three helpers, would be able to cope with the work of handling four teams.

7. Role of the instructor

The work of the instructor is most important and the success or failure of the exercise depends to a large extent on his ability to carry out his many tasks. Besides being in over-all charge of the course he will, in most cases, also have to take on the role of management bargainer. In that position he shall function as the chief opponent to the union teams, performing as realistically as possible the same work as the management negotiator would do in a real case. For his guidance he shall have to rely on the specific information concerning management position contained in the case description. In the case that a competent person other than the instructor is available to play the role of management negotiatior such an arrangement would normally be advantageous. The instructor would then have more time for overseeing the whole operation and the progress of the work.

The whole exercise is based on the assumption that the teams will be able to complete their assignments and have a concluded new agreement ready at the end of the team work phase. These agreements shall then be analysed and their contents and, in particular, their differences be used to illustrate various points in the following discussion.

It is essential that the management bargainer exercises as complete impartiality in dealing with the different teams as possible, treating all claims strictly according to their financial and other implications to the company and making concessions only after careful estimation of what the likely results to the company may be. In this way the final discussion/evaluation of the exercise can be held without participants feeling that irrelevant factors have influenced the quality of any of the agreements reached.

In the opening session each team shall receive identical proposals for changes in the collective agreement from the management. Deviation from these opening suggestions may later be made in accordance with the progress of the talks with each team and in keeping with the principle of give and take. When summarised at the end the total of gains on the one hand and concessions made on the other should come out to be as close to equal for all the teams as possible.

8. Work of the teams

The main purpose of the whole exercise is to provide, as realistically as possible, a true picture of the work of a union bargaining committee. The teams should therefore be encouraged and assisted in undertaking the same work as a trade union bargaining committee might be charged with in a real bargaining.

The first task of each team will thus be to prepare, separately, a list of claims for submission to the management at the opening session. The basic structure of these claims have already been discussed and agreed on in the union meeting referred to in the case description. These terms will therefore has to serve as guidelines and basis for the teams. This should not, however, prevent the teams from discussing and formulating such additional proposals a team may feel justified and to be within its power to accomplish.

In this connection a helper may occasionally have to warn a team of the need for a realistic approach in its formulation of claims. There will always be a limit to what an undertaking can accept in respect of increased labour costs, and even though the first duty of a union always must be to improve the living and working conditions for its members, this other aspect will also have to be borne in mind if it shall be possible to conclude any collective bargaining with a prospect of success.

To provide a basis for its discussion with management a bargaining committee will have to devote much of its work to estimating and calculating financial and other implications of both its own claims and of proposals made by the management. This may be a rather tedious task, not always very much appreciated or even well-mastered by trade union negotiators. All too often, however, a bargaining committee finds itself lacking the evidence with which it would have been possible to prove a particular point in the discussions with the management. This evidence might have been available at the right moment had only proper preparations been made. Such aspects of collective bargaining often need to be emphasised and sufficient time be allocated for training in the field.

Collecting and using documentary material and data in support of union views and claims as well as to illustrate and prove consequences of management proposals is also an important field of collective bargaining preparations which should be included in the exercise. Such documentation may include various forms of official publications, in particular material relevant to labour matters such as wages, prices, employment, productivity, market position in the industry, etc. Company annual reports provide another valuable source of information in which it is usually possible to find information regarding the financial position of the undertaking concerned, its sales and prices, market situation and, in particular, profits and dividends.

9.   Bargaining_sessions

As soon as each team has completed its initial preparatory work the bargaining sessions shall begin.

These will consist of a number of successive meetings between the management and each team separately in which the issues will be systematically discussed with arguments for and against produced.

In the intervals between the meetings the teams discuss and review the progress of the talks, produce and survey documentation and consider in which ways, if any, it may be possible for the team to make adjustments in its stand on any issue for the purpose of reducing the distance in position between the team and the management. Meanwhile the management continues to meet and discuss with the other teams.

In a real case this succession of meetings with argumentation, concessions and compromises might continue, if need be, for quite some time with shorter or longer intervals until the differences are reduced to such an extent that an agreement is reached. Alternatively, the parties would not be able to adjust their positions enough to reach an agreement and the whole session would end in deadlock. In this exercise we do not have all the time that may be required in a real case at our disposal and it will therefore be necessary to set a deadline at which all the teams shall have to have the bargaining completed. It will then be the joint responsibility of all the teams, with the assistance of the helpers if need be, to make sure the work is finished on time without a need for an abrupt interruption before the argumentation and compromising is actually exhausted.

10.   Evaluation_of_methods_and_results

The final session shall be used for an evaluation of the whole exercise, its methods and degree of success. This may be best accomplished by starting with a comparison of the objectives of each team, the tactics applied to solve the existing problem and finally how the team did solve the problem.

This will in most cases provide a good illustration to the fact that even when existing conditions are very similar - in this case actually identical - the interpretation of the situation will vary between different persons and groups. So will priorities and consequently also the tactics to be used, and this will finally lead to different results in solving the actual problem. The best result is the one that meets the workers' interests most completely, directly as well as in the long run.

The evaluation will be greatly facilitated if all the agreements are typed and distributed to all participants before the session starts.

ANNEX 2.C

Some short exercises that might be based on the above case

All the exercises suggested below can be done by individuals, in groups or by the class as a whole with the aid of the instructor.

(1) List the most effective points which might be made by management in resisting union claims. Evaluate their strength in some way, for example by allotting them a value from 1 to 5.

(2) List the most effective points that might be made by the union. Evaluate them.

(3) Briefly note the arguments that might be used to counter the employer's points.

(4) Briefly note the arguments most likely to be used by management to counter the union's points.

(5) Discuss those arguments frankly and suggest counterpoints.

(6) Draw up concrete proposals for inclusion in a revised collective agreement. Defend these in group or class discussion.

(7) Prepare the general secretary's opening statement for the first meeting with the employers.

(8) Role-play the negotiations to the extent that time permits.

(9) Role-play a union committee meeting to report the outcome.

ANNEX 3

ILO Conventions and Recommendations
concerning collective bargaining

Convention 87

CONVENTION CONCERNING
FREEDOM OF ASSOCIATION AND PROTECTION OF
THE RIGHT TO ORGANISE

The General Conference of the International Labour Organisation,

Having been convened at San Francisco by the Governing Body of the International Labour Office, and having met in its Thirty-first Session on 17 June 1948 ;

Having decided to adopt, in the form of a Convention, certain proposals concerning freedom of association and protection of the right to organise, which is the seventh item on the agenda of the session ;

Considering that the Preamble to the Constitution of the International Labour Organisation declares " recognition of the principle of freedom of association " to be a means of improving conditions of labour and of establishing peace ;

Considering that the Declaration of Philadelphia reaffirms that " freedom of expression and of association are essential to sustained progress " ;

Considering that the International Labour Conference, at its Thirtieth Session, unanimously adopted the principles which should form the basis for international regulation ;

Considering that the General Assembly of the United Nations, at its Second Session, endorsed these principles and requested the International Labour Organisation to continue every effort in order that it may be possible to adopt one or several international Conventions ;

adopts this ninth day of July of the year one thousand nine hundred and forty-eight the following Convention, which may be cited as the Freedom of Association and Protection of the Right to Organise Convention, 1948 :

PART I. FREEDOM OF ASSOCIATION

Article 1

Each Member of the International Labour Organisation for which this Convention is in force undertakes to give effect to the following provisions.

Article 2

Workers and employers, without distinction whatsoever, shall have the right to establish and, subject only to the rules of the organisation concerned, to join organisations of their own choosing without previous authorisation.

Article 3

1. Workers' and employers' organisations shall have the right to draw up their constitutions and rules, to elect their representatives in full

freedom, to organise their administration and activities and to formulate their programmes.

2. The public authorities shall refrain from any interference which would restrict this right or impede the lawful exercise thereof.

Article 4

Workers' and employers' organisations shall not be liable to be dissolved or suspended by administrative authority.

Article 5

Workers' and employers' organisations shall have the right to establish and join federations and confederations and any such organisation, federation or confederation shall have the right to affiliate with international organisations of workers and employers.

Article 6

The provisions of Articles 2, 3 and 4 hereof apply to federations and confederations of workers' and employers' organisations.

Article 7

The acquisition of legal personality by workers' and employers' organisations, federations and confederations shall not be made subject to conditions of such a character as to restrict the application of the provisions of Articles 2, 3 and 4 hereof.

Article 8

1. In exercising the rights provided for in this Convention workers and employers and their respective organisations, like other persons or organised collectivities, shall respect the law of the land.

2. The law of the land shall not be such as to impair, nor shall it be so applied as to impair, the guarantees provided for in this Convention.

Article 9

1. The extent to which the guarantees provided for in this Convention shall apply to the armed forces and the police shall be determined by national laws or regulations.

2. In accordance with the principle set forth in paragraph 8 of Article 19 of the Constitution of the International Labour Organisation the ratification of this Convention by any Member shall not be deemed to affect any existing law, award, custom or agreement in virtue of which members of the armed forces or the police enjoy any right guaranteed by this Convention.

Article 10

In this Convention the term " organisation " means any organisation of workers or of employers for furthering and defending the interests of workers or of employers.

PART II. PROTECTION OF THE RIGHT TO ORGANISE

Article 11

Each Member of the International Labour Organisation for which this Convention is in force undertakes to take all necessary and appropriate measures to ensure that workers and employers may exercise freely the right to organise.

PART III. MISCELLANEOUS PROVISIONS

Article 12

1. In respect of the territories referred to in Article 35 of the Constitution of the International Labour Organisation as amended by the Constitution of the International Labour Organisation Instrument of Amendment, 1946, other than the territories referred to in paragraphs 4 and 5 of the said Article as so amended, each Member of the Organisation which ratifies this Convention shall communicate to the Director-General of the International Labour Office with or as soon as possible after its ratification a declaration stating—

(a) the territories in respect of which it undertakes that the provisions of the Convention shall be applied without modification ;

(b) the territories in respect of which it undertakes that the provisions of the Convention shall be applied subject to modifications, together with details of the said modifications ;

(c) the territories in respect of which the Convention is inapplicable and in such cases the grounds on which it is inapplicable ;

(d) the territories in respect of which it reserves its decision.

2. The undertakings referred to in subparagraphs *(a)* and *(b)* of paragraph 1 of this Article shall be deemed to be an integral part of the ratification and shall have the force of ratification.

3. Any Member may at any time by a subsequent declaration cancel in whole or in part any reservations made in its original declaration in virtue of subparagraphs *(b)*, *(c)* or *(d)* of paragraph 1 of this Article.

4. Any Member may, at any time at which this Convention is subject to denunciation in accordance with the provisions of Article 16, communicate to the Director-General a declaration modifying in any other respect the terms of any former declaration and stating the present position in respect of such territories as it may specify.

Article 13

1. Where the subject-matter of this Convention is within the self-governing powers of any non-metropolitan territory, the Member responsible for the international relations of that territory may, in agreement with the government of the territory, communicate to the Director-General of the International Labour Office a declaration accepting on behalf of the territory the obligations of this Convention.

2.   A declaration accepting the obligations of this Convention may be communicated to the Director-General of the International Labour Office—

(a)   by two or more Members of the Organisation in respect of any territory which is under their joint authority ; or

(b)   by any international authority responsible for the administration of any territory, in virtue of the Charter of the United Nations or otherwise, in respect of any such territory.

3.   Declarations communicated to the Director-General of the International Labour Office in accordance with the preceding paragraphs of this Article shall indicate whether the provisions of the Convention will be applied in the territory concerned without modification or subject to modifications ; when the declaration indicates that the provisions of the Convention will be applied subject to modifications it shall give details of the said modifications.

4.   The Member, Members or international authority concerned may at any time by a subsequent declaration renounce in whole or in part the right to have recourse to any modification indicated in any former declaration.

5.   The Member, Members or international authority concerned may, at any time at which this Convention is subject to denunciation in accordance with the provisions of Article 16, communicate to the Director-General of the International Labour Office a declaration modifying in any other respect the terms of any former declaration and stating the present position in respect of the application of the Convention.

PART IV. FINAL PROVISIONS

Article 14

The formal ratifications of this Convention shall be communicated to the Director-General of the International Labour Office for registration.

Article 15

1.   This Convention shall be binding only upon those Members of the International Labour Organisation whose ratifications have been registered with the Director-General.

2.   It shall come into force twelve months after the date on which the ratifications of two Members have been registered with the Director-General.

3.   Thereafter, this Convention shall come into force for any Member twelve months after the date on which its ratification has been registered.

Article 16

1.   A Member which has ratified this Convention may denounce it after the expiration of ten years from the date on which the Convention first comes into force, by an act communicated to the Director-General of the International Labour Office for registration.   Such denunciation shall not take effect until one year after the date on which it is registered.

2.   Each Member which has ratified this Convention and which does not, within the year following the expiration of the period of ten years mentioned in the preceding paragraph, exercise the right of denunciation provided for in this Article, will be bound for another period of ten years and, thereafter, may denounce this Convention at the expiration of each period of ten years under the terms provided for in this Article.

Article 17

1.   The Director-General of the International Labour Office shall notify all Members of the International Labour Organisation of the registration of all ratifications, declarations and denunciations communicated to him by the Members of the Organisation.

2.   When notifying the Members of the Organisation of the registration of the second ratification communicated to him, the Director-General shall draw the attention of the Members of the Organisation to the date upon which the Convention will come into force.

Article 18

The Director-General of the International Labour Office shall communicate to the Secretary-General of the United Nations for registration in accordance with Article 102 of the Charter of the United Nations full particulars of all ratifications, declarations and acts of denunciation registered by him in accordance with the provisions of the preceding articles.

Article 19

At the expiration of each period of ten years after the coming into force of this Convention, the Governing Body of the International Labour Office shall present to the General Conference a report on the working of this Convention and shall consider the desirability of placing on the agenda of the Conference the question of its revision in whole or in part.

Article 20

1.   Should the Conference adopt a new Convention revising this Convention in whole or in part, then, unless the new Convention otherwise provides,

(a)   the ratification by a Member of the new revising Convention shall *ipso jure* involve the immediate denunciation of this Convention, notwithstanding the provisions of Article 16 above, if and when the new revising Convention shall have come into force ;

(b)   as from the date when the new revising Convention comes into force this Convention shall cease to be open to ratification by the Members.

2.   This Convention shall in any case remain in force in its actual form and content for those Members which have ratified it but have not ratified the revising Convention.

Article 21

The English and French versions of the text of this Convention are equally authoritative.

CONVENTION No. 98

Convention concerning the Application of the Principles of the Right to Organise and to Bargain Collectively

The General Conference of the International Labour Organisation,

Having been convened at Geneva by the Governing Body of the International Labour Office, and having met in its Thirty-second Session on 8 June 1949, and

Having decided upon the adoption of certain proposals concerning the application of the principles of the right to organise and to bargain collectively, which is the fourth item on the agenda of the session, and

Having determined that these proposals shall take the form of an international Convention,

adopts this first day of July of the year one thousand nine hundred and forty-nine the following Convention, which may be cited as the Right to Organise and Collective Bargaining Convention, 1949 :

Article 1

1. Workers shall enjoy adequate protection against acts of anti-union discrimination in respect of their employment.

2. Such protection shall apply more particularly in respect of acts calculated to—

(a) make the employment of a worker subject to the condition that he shall not, join a union or shall relinquish trade union membership ;

(b) cause the dismissal of or otherwise prejudice a worker by reason of union membership or because of participation in union activities outside working hours or, with the consent of the employer, within working hours.

Article 2

1. Workers' and employers' organisations shall enjoy adequate protection against any acts of interference by each other or each other's agents or members in their establishment, functioning or administration.

2. In particular, acts which are designed to promote the establishment of workers' organisations under the domination of employers' organisations, or to support workers' organisations by financial or other means, with the object of placing such organisations under the control of employers or employers' organisations, shall be deemed to constitute acts of interference within the meaning of this Article.

Article 3

Machinery appropriate to national conditions shall be established, where necessary, for the purpose of ensuring respect for the right to organise as defined in the preceding Articles.

Article 4

Measures appropriate to national conditions shall be taken, where necessary, to encourage and promote the full development and utilisation of machinery for voluntary negotiation between employers or employers' organisations and workers' organisations, with a view to the regulation of terms and conditions of employment by means of collective agreements.

Article 5

1. The extent to which the guarantees provided for in this Convention shall apply to the armed forces and the police shall be determined by national laws or regulations.

2. In accordance with the principle set forth in paragraph 8 of article 19 of the Constitution of the International Labour Organisation the ratification of this Convention by any Member shall not be deemed to affect any existing law, award, custom or agreement in virtue of which members of the armed forces or the police enjoy any right guaranteed by this Convention.

Article 6

This Convention does not deal with the position of public servants engaged in the administration of the State, nor shall it be construed as prejudicing their rights or status in any way.

Article 7

The formal ratifications of this Convention shall be communicated to the Director-General of the International Labour Office for registration.

Article 8

1. This Convention shall be binding only upon those Members of the International Labour Organisation whose ratifications have been registered with the Director-General.

2. It shall come into force twelve months after the date on which the ratifications of two Members have been registered with the Director-General.

3. Thereafter, this Convention shall come into force for any Member twelve months after the date on which its ratification has been registered.

Article 9

1. Declarations communicated to the Director-General of the International Labour Office in accordance with paragraph 2 of article 35 of the Constitution of the International Labour Organisation shall indicate—

(a) the territories in respect of which the Member concerned undertakes that the provisions of the Convention shall be applied without modification ;

(b) the territories in respect of which it undertakes that the provisions of the Convention shall be applied subject to modifications, together with details of the said modifications ;

(c) the territories in respect of which the Convention is inapplicable and in such cases the grounds on which it is inapplicable ;

(d) the territories in respect of which it reserves its decision pending further consideration of the position.

2. The undertakings referred to in subparagraphs (a) and (b) of paragraph 1 of this Article shall be deemed to be an integral part of the ratification and shall have the force of ratification.

3. Any Member may at any time by a subsequent declaration cancel in whole or in part any reservation made in its original declaration in virtue of subparagraph (b), (c) or (d) of paragraph 1 of this Article.

4. Any Member may, at any time at which the Convention is subject to denunciation in accordance with the provisions of Article 11, communicate to

the Director-General a declaration modifying in any other respect the terms of any former declaration and stating the present position in respect of such territories as it may specify.

Article 10

1. Declarations communicated to the Director-General of the International Labour Office in accordance with paragraph 4 or 5 of article 35 of the Constitution of the International Labour Organisation shall indicate whether the provisions of the Convention will be applied in the territory concerned without modification or subject to modifications ; when the declaration indicates that the provisions of the Convention will be applied subject to modifications, it shall give details of the said modifications.

2. The Member, Members or international authority concerned may at any time by a subsequent declaration renounce in whole or in part the right to have recourse to any modification indicated in any former declaration.

3. The Member, Members or international authority concerned may, at any time at which this Convention is subject to denunciation in accordance with the provisions of Article 11, communicate to the Director-General a declaration modifying in any other respect the terms of any former declaration and stating the present position in respect of the application of the Convention.

Article 11

1. A Member which has ratified this Convention may denounce it after the expiration of ten years from the date on which the Convention first comes into force, by an act communicated to the Director-General of the International Labour Office for registration. Such denunciation shall not take effect until one year after the date on which it is registered.

2. Each Member which has ratified this Convention and which does not, within the year following the expiration of the period of ten years mentioned in the preceding paragraph, exercise the right of denunciation provided for in this Article, will be bound for another period of ten years and, thereafter, may denounce this Convention at the expiration of each period of ten years under the terms provided for in this Article.

Article 12

1. The Director-General of the International Labour Office shall notify all Members of the International Labour Organisation of the registration of all ratifications, declarations and denunciations communicated to him by the Members of the Organisation.

2. When notifying the Members of the Organisation of the registration of the second ratification communicated to him, the Director-General shall draw the attention of the Members of the Organisation to the date upon which the Convention will come into force.

Article 13

The Director-General of the International Labour Office shall communicate to the Secretary-General of the United Nations for registration in accordance with Article 102 of the Charter of the United Nations full particulars of all ratifications, declarations and acts of denunciation registered by him in accordance with the provisions of the preceding Articles.

Article 14

At such times as it may consider necessary the Governing Body of the International Labour Office shall present to the General Conference a report on the working of this Convention and shall examine the desirability of placing on the agenda of the Conference the question of its revision in whole or in part.

Article 15

1. Should the Conference adopt a new Convention revising this Convention in whole or in part, then, unless the new Convention otherwise provides,

(a) the ratification by a Member of the new revising Convention shall *ipso jure* involve the immediate denunciation of this Convention, notwithstanding the provisions of Article 11 above, if and when the new revising Convention shall have come into force ;

(b) as from the date when the new revising Convention comes into force, this Convention shall cease to be open to ratification by the Members.

2. This Convention shall in any case remain in force in its actual form and content for those Members which have ratified it but have not ratified the revising Convention.

Article 16

The English and French versions of the text of this Convention are equally authoritative.

Convention 135

CONVENTION CONCERNING PROTECTION AND FACILITIES TO BE AFFORDED TO WORKERS' REPRESENTATIVES IN THE UNDERTAKING

The General Conference of the International Labour Organisation,

Having been convened at Geneva by the Governing Body of the International Labour Office, and having met in its Fifty-sixth Session on 2 June 1971, and

Noting the terms of the Right to Organise and Collective Bargaining Convention, 1949, which provides for protection of workers against acts of anti-union discrimination in respect of their employment, and

Considering that it is desirable to supplement these terms with respect to workers' representatives, and

Having decided upon the adoption of certain proposals with regard to protection and facilities afforded to workers' representatives in the undertaking, which is the fifth item on the agenda of the session, and

Having determined that these proposals shall take the form of an international Convention,

adopts this twenty-third day of June of the year one thousand nine hundred and seventy-one the following Convention, which may be cited as the Workers' Representatives Convention, 1971:

Article 1

Workers' representatives in the undertaking shall enjoy effective protection against any act prejudicial to them, including dismissal, based on their status or activities as a workers' representative or on union membership or participation in union activities, in so far as they act in conformity with existing laws or collective agreements or other jointly agreed arrangements.

Article 2

1. Such facilities in the undertaking shall be afforded to workers' representatives as may be appropriate in order to enable them to carry out their functions promptly and efficiently.

2. In this connection account shall be taken of the characteristics of the industrial relations system of the country and the needs, size and capabilities of the undertaking concerned.

3. The granting of such facilities shall not impair the efficient operation of the undertaking concerned.

Article 3

For the purpose of this Convention the term " workers' representatives " means persons who are recognised as such under national law or practice, whether they are—

(a) trade union representatives, namely, representatives designated or elected by trade unions or by the members of such unions; or *(b)* elected representatives, namely, representatives who are freely elected by the workers of the undertaking in accordance with provisions of national laws or regulations or of collective agreements and whose functions do not include activities which are recognised as the exclusive prerogative of trade unions in the country concerned.

Article 4

National laws or regulations, collective agreements, arbitration awards or court decisions may determine the type or types of workers' representatives which shall be entitled to the protection and facilities provided for in this Convention.

Article 5

Where there exist in the same undertaking both trade union representatives and elected representatives, appropriate measures shall be taken, wherever necessary, to ensure that the existence of elected representatives is not used to undermine the position of the trade unions concerned or their representatives and to encourage co-operation on all relevant matters between the elected representatives and the trade unions concerned and their representatives.

Article 6

Effect may be given to this Convention through national laws or regulations or collective agreements, or in any other manner consistent with national practice.

Article 7

The formal ratifications of this Convention shall be communicated to the Director-General of the International Labour Office for registration.

Article 8

1. This Convention shall be binding only upon those Members of the International Labour Organisation whose ratifications have been registered with the Director-General.

2. It shall come into force twelve months after the date on which the ratifications of two Members have been registered with the Director-General.

3. Thereafter, this Convention shall come into force for any Member twelve months after the date on which its ratification has been registered.

Article 9

1. A Member which has ratified this Convention may denounce it after the expiration of ten years from the date on which the Convention first comes into force, by an act communicated to the Director-General of the International Labour Office for registration. Such denunciation shall not take effect until one year after the date on which it is registered.

2. Each Member which has ratified this Convention and which does not, within the year following the expiration of the period of ten years mentioned in the preceding paragraph, exercise the right of denunciation provided for in this Article, will be

bound for another period of ten years and, thereafter, may denounce this Convention at the expiration of each period of ten years under the terms provided for in this Article.

Article 10

1. The Director-General of the International Labour Office shall notify all Members of the International Labour Organisation of the registration of all ratifications and denunciations communicated to him by the Members of the Organisation.

2. When notifying the Members of the Organisation of the registration of the second ratification communicated to him, the Director-General shall draw the attention of the Members of the Organisation to the date upon which the Convention will come into force.

Article 11

The Director-General of the International Labour Office shall communicate to the Secretary-General of the United Nations for registration in accordance with Article 102 of the Charter of the United Nations full particulars of all ratifications and acts of denunciation registered by him in accordance with the provisions of the preceding Articles.

Article 12

At such times as it may consider necessary the Governing Body of the International Labour Office shall present to the General Conference a report on the working of this Convention and shall examine the desirability of placing on the agenda of the Conference the question of its revision in whole or in part.

Article 13

1. Should the Conference adopt a new Convention revising this Convention in whole or in part, then, unless the new Convention otherwise provides—

(a) the ratification by a Member of the new revising Convention shall *ipso jure* involve the immediate denunciation of this Convention, notwithstanding the provisions of Article 9 above, if and when the new revising Convention shall have come into force;

(b) as from the date when the new revising Convention comes into force this Convention shall cease to be open to ratification by the Members.

2. This Convention shall in any case remain in force in its actual form and content for those Members which have ratified it but have not ratified the revising Convention.

Article 14

The English and French versions of the text of this Convention are equally authoritative.

Convention 150

CONVENTION CONCERNING LABOUR ADMINISTRATION: ROLE, FUNCTIONS AND ORGANISATION

The General Conference of the International Labour Organisation,

Having been convened at Geneva by the Governing Body of the International Labour Office, and having met in its Sixty-fourth Session on 7 June 1978, and

Recalling the terms of existing international labour Conventions and Recommendations, including in particular the Labour Inspection Convention, 1947, the Labour Inspection (Agriculture) Convention, 1969, and the Employment Service Convention, 1948, which call for the exercise of particular labour administration activities, and

Considering it desirable to adopt instruments establishing guidelines regarding the over-all system of labour administration, and

Recalling the terms of the Employment Policy Convention, 1964, and of the Human Resources Development Convention, 1975; recalling also the goal of the creation of full and adequately remunerated employment and affirming the need for programmes of labour administration to work towards this goal and to give effect to the objectives of the said Conventions, and

Recognising the necessity of fully respecting the autonomy of employers' and workers' organisations, recalling in this connection the terms of existing international labour Conventions and Recommendations guaranteeing rights of association, organisation and collective bargaining—and particularly the Freedom of Association and Protection of the Right to Organise Convention, 1948, and the Right to Organise and Collective Bargaining Convention, 1949—which forbid any interference by public authorities which would restrict these rights or impede the lawful exercise thereof, and considering that employers' and workers' organisations have essential roles in attaining the objectives of economic, social and cultural progress, and

Having decided upon the adoption of certain proposals with regard to labour administration: role, functions and organisation, which is the fourth item on the agenda of the session, and

Having determined that these proposals shall take the form of an international Convention,

adopts this twenty-sixth day of June of the year one thousand nine hundred and seventy-eight the following Convention, which may be cited as the Labour Administration Convention, 1978:

Article 1

For the purpose of this Convention—

(a) the term " labour administration " means public administration activities in the field of national labour policy;

(b) the term " system of labour administration " covers all public administration bodies responsible for and/or engaged in labour administration—whether they are ministerial departments or public agencies, including parastatal and regional

or local agencies or any other form of decentralised administration—and any institutional framework for the co-ordination of the activities of such bodies and for consultation with and participation by employers and workers and their organisations.

Article 2

A Member which ratifies this Convention may, in accordance with national laws or regulations, or national practice, delegate or entrust certain activities of labour administration to non-governmental organisations, particularly employers' and workers' organisations, or—where appropriate—to employers' and workers' representatives.

Article 3

A Member which ratifies this Convention may regard particular activities in the field of its national labour policy as being matters which, in accordance with national laws or regulations, or national practice, are regulated by having recourse to direct negotiations between employers' and workers' organisations.

Article 4

Each Member which ratifies this Convention shall, in a manner appropriate to national conditions, ensure the organisation and effective operation in its territory of a system of labour administration, the functions and responsibilities of which are properly co-ordinated.

Article 5

1. Each Member which ratifies this Convention shall make arrangements appropriate to national conditions to secure, within the system of labour administration, consultation, co-operation and negotiation between the public authorities and the most representative organisations of employers and workers, or—where appropriate— employers' and workers' representatives.

2. To the extent compatible with national laws and regulations, and national practice, such arrangements shall be made at the national, regional and local levels as well as at the level of the different sectors of economic activity.

Article 6

1. The competent bodies within the system of labour administration shall, as appropriate, be responsible for or contribute to the preparation, administration, co-ordination, checking and review of national labour policy, and be the instrument within the ambit of public administration for the preparation and implementation of laws and regulations giving effect thereto.

2. In particular, these bodies, taking into account relevant international labour standards, shall—

(a) participate in the preparation, administration, co-ordination, checking and review of national employment policy, in accordance with national laws and regulations, and national practice;

(b) study and keep under review the situation of employed, unemployed and under-employed persons, taking into account national laws and regulations and national practice concerning conditions of work and working life and terms of employment, draw attention to defects and abuses in such conditions and terms and submit proposals on means to overcome them;

(c) make their services available to employers and workers, and their respective organisations, as may be appropriate under national laws or regulations, or national practice, with a view to the promotion—at national, regional and local levels as well as at the level of the different sectors of economic activity—of effective consultation and co-operation between public authorities and bodies and employers' and workers' organisations, as well as between such organisations;

(d) make technical advice available to employers and workers and their respective organisations on their request.

Article 7

When national conditions so require, with a view to meeting the needs of the largest possible number of workers, and in so far as such activities are not already covered, each Member which ratifies this Convention shall promote the extension, by gradual stages if necessary, of the functions of the system of labour administration to include activities, to be carried out in co-operation with other competent bodies, relating to the conditions of work and working life of appropriate categories of workers who are not, in law, employed persons, such as—

(a) tenants who do not engage outside help, sharecroppers and similar categories of agricultural workers;

(b) self-employed workers who do not engage outside help, occupied in the informal sector as understood in national practice;

(c) members of co-operatives and worker-managed undertakings;

(d) persons working under systems established by communal customs or traditions.

Article 8

To the extent compatible with national laws and regulations and national practice, the competent bodies within the system of labour administration shall contribute to the preparation of national policy concerning international labour affairs, participate in the representation of the State with respect to such affairs and contribute to the preparation of measures to be taken at the national level with respect thereto.

Article 9

With a view to the proper co-ordination of the functions and responsibilities of the system of labour administration, in a manner determined by national laws or regulations, or national practice, a ministry of labour or another comparable body shall have the means to ascertain whether any parastatal agencies which may be responsible for particular labour administration activities, and any regional or local agencies to which particular labour administration activities may have been delegated, are operating in accordance with national laws and regulations and are adhering to the objectives assigned to them.

Article 10

1. The staff of the labour administration system shall be composed of persons who are suitably qualified for the activities to which they are assigned, who have access to training necessary for such activities and who are independent of improper external influences.

2. Such staff shall have the status, the material means and the financial resources necessary for the effective performance of their duties.

Article 11

The formal ratifications of this Convention shall be communicated to the Director-General of the International Labour Office for registration.

Article 12

1. This Convention shall be binding only upon those Members of the International Labour Organisation whose ratifications have been registered with the Director-General.

2. It shall come into force twelve months after the date on which the ratifications of two Members have been registered with the Director-General.

3. Thereafter, this Convention shall come into force for any Member twelve months after the date on which its ratification has been registered.

Article 13

1. A Member which has ratified this Convention may denounce it after the expiration of ten years from the date on which the Convention first comes into force, by an act communicated to the Director-General of the International Labour Office for registration. Such denunciation shall not take effect until one year after the date on which it is registered.

2. Each Member which has ratified this Convention and which does not, within the year following the expiration of the period of ten years mentioned in the preceding paragraph, exercise the right of denunciation provided for in this Article, will be bound for another period of ten years and, thereafter, may denounce this Convention at the expiration of each period of ten years under the terms provided for in this Article.

Article 14

1. The Director-General of the International Labour Office shall notify all Members of the International Labour Organisation of the registration of all ratifications and denunciations communicated to him by the Members of the Organisation.

2. When notifying the Members of the Organisation of the registration of the second ratification communicated to him, the Director-General shall draw the attention of the Members of the Organisation to the date upon which the Convention will come into force.

Article 15

The Director-General of the International Labour Office shall communicate to the Secretary-General of the United Nations for registration in accordance with Article 102 of the Charter of the United Nations full particulars of all ratifications and acts of denunciation registered by him in accordance with the provisions of the preceding Articles.

Article 16

At such times as it may consider necessary the Governing Body of the International Labour Office shall present to the General Conference a report on the working of this Convention and shall examine the desirability of placing on the agenda of the Conference the question of its revision in whole or in part.

Article 17

1. Should the Conference adopt a new Convention revising this Convention in whole or in part, then, unless the new Convention otherwise provides—

(a) the ratification by a Member of the new revising Convention shall *ipso jure* involve the immediate denunciation of this Convention, notwithstanding the provisions of Article 13 above, if and when the new revising Convention shall have come into force;

(b) as from the date when the new revising Convention comes into force this Convention shall cease to be open to ratification by the Members.

2. This Convention shall in any case remain in force in its actual form and content for those Members which have ratified it but have not ratified the revising Convention.

Article 18

The English and French versions of the text of this Convention are equally authoritative.

Convention 151

CONVENTION CONCERNING PROTECTION OF THE RIGHT TO ORGANISE AND PROCEDURES FOR DETERMINING CONDITIONS OF EMPLOYMENT IN THE PUBLIC SERVICE

The General Conference of the International Labour Organisation,

Having been convened at Geneva by the Governing Body of the International Labour Office, and having met in its Sixty-fourth Session on 7 June 1978, and

Noting the terms of the Freedom of Association and Protection of the Right to Organise Convention, 1948, the Right to Organise and Collective Bargaining Convention, 1949, and the Workers' Representatives Convention and Recommendation, 1971, and

Recalling that the Right to Organise and Collective Bargaining Convention, 1949, does not cover certain categories of public employees and that the Workers' Representatives Convention and Recommendation, 1971, apply to workers' representatives in the undertaking, and

Noting the considerable expansion of public-service activities in many countries and the need for sound labour relations between public authorities and public employees' organisations, and

Having regard to the great diversity of political, social and economic systems among member States and the differences in practice among them (e.g. as to the respective functions of central and local government, of federal, state and provincial authorities, and of state-owned undertakings and various types of autonomous or semi-autonomous public bodies, as well as to the nature of employment relationships), and

Taking into account the particular problems arising as to the scope of, and definitions for the purpose of, any international instrument, owing to the differences in many countries between private and public employment, as well as the difficulties of interpretation which have arisen in respect of the application of relevant provisions of the Right to Organise and Collective Bargaining Convention, 1949, to public servants, and the observations of the supervisory bodies of the ILO on a number of occasions that some governments have applied these provisions in a manner which excludes large groups of public employees from coverage by that Convention, and

Having decided upon the adoption of certain proposals with regard to freedom of association and procedures for determining conditions of employment in the public service, which is the fifth item on the agenda of the session, and

Having determined that these proposals shall take the form of an international Convention,

adopts this twenty-seventh day of June of the year one thousand nine hundred and seventy-eight the following Convention, which may be cited as the Labour Relations (Public Service) Convention, 1978:

PART I. SCOPE AND DEFINITIONS

Article 1

1. This Convention applies to all persons employed by public authorities, to the extent that more favourable provisions in other international labour Conventions are not applicable to them.

2. The extent to which the guarantees provided for in this Convention shall apply to high-level employees whose functions are normally considered as policy-making or managerial, or to employees whose duties are of a highly confidential nature, shall be determined by national laws or regulations.

3. The extent to which the guarantees provided for in this Convention shall apply to the armed forces and the police shall be determined by national laws or regulations.

Article 2

For the purpose of this Convention, the term " public employee " means any person covered by the Convention in accordance with Article 1 thereof.

Article 3

For the purpose of this Convention, the term " public employees' organisation " means any organisation, however composed, the purpose of which is to further and defend the interests of public employees.

PART II. PROTECTION OF THE RIGHT TO ORGANISE

Article 4

1. Public employees shall enjoy adequate protection against acts of anti-union discrimination in respect of their employment.

2. Such protection shall apply more particularly in respect of acts calculated to—

(a) make the employment of public employees subject to the condition that they shall not join or shall relinquish membership of a public employees' organisation;

(b) cause the dismissal of or otherwise prejudice a public employee by reason of membership of a public employees' organisation or because of participation in the normal activities of such an organisation.

Article 5

1. Public employees' organisations shall enjoy complete independence from public authorities.

2. Public employees' organisations shall enjoy adequate protection against any acts of interference by a public authority in their establishment, functioning or administration.

3. In particular, acts which are designed to promote the establishment of public employees' organisations under the domination of a public authority, or to support

public employees' organisations by financial or other means, with the object of placing such organisations under the control of a public authority, shall be deemed to constitute acts of interference within the meaning of this Article.

PART III. FACILITIES TO BE AFFORDED TO PUBLIC EMPLOYEES' ORGANISATIONS

Article 6

1. Such facilities shall be afforded to the representatives of recognised public employees' organisations as may be appropriate in order to enable them to carry out their functions promptly and efficiently, both during and outside their hours of work.

2. The granting of such facilities shall not impair the efficient operation of the administration or service concerned.

3. The nature and scope of these facilities shall be determined in accordance with the methods referred to in Article 7 of this Convention, or by other appropriate means.

PART IV. PROCEDURES FOR DETERMINING TERMS AND CONDITIONS OF EMPLOYMENT

Article 7

Measures appropriate to national conditions shall be taken, where necessary, to encourage and promote the full development and utilisation of machinery for negotiation of terms and conditions of employment between the public authorities concerned and public employees' organisations, or of such other methods as will allow representatives of public employees to participate in the determination of these matters.

PART V. SETTLEMENT OF DISPUTES

Article 8

The settlement of disputes arising in connection with the determination of terms and conditions of employment shall be sought, as may be appropriate to national conditions, through negotiation between the parties or through independent and impartial machinery, such as mediation, conciliation and arbitration, established in such a manner as to ensure the confidence of the parties involved.

PART VI. CIVIL AND POLITICAL RIGHTS

Article 9

Public employees shall have, as other workers, the civil and political rights which are essential for the normal exercise of freedom of association, subject only to the obligations arising from their status and the nature of their functions.

PART VII. FINAL PROVISIONS

Article 10

The formal ratifications of this Convention shall be communicated to the Director-General of the International Labour Office for registration.

Article 11

1. This Convention shall be binding only upon those Members of the International Labour Organisation whose ratifications have been registered with the Director-General.

2. It shall come into force twelve months after the date on which the ratifications of two Members have been registered with the Director-General.

3. Thereafter, this Convention shall come into force for any Member twelve months after the date on which its ratification has been registered.

Article 12

1. A Member which has ratified this Convention may denounce it after the expiration of ten years from the date on which the Convention first comes into force, by an act communicated to the Director-General of the International Labour Office for registration. Such denunciation shall not take effect until one year after the date on which it is registered.

2. Each Member which has ratified this Convention and which does not, within the year following the expiration of the period of ten years mentioned in the preceding paragraph, exercise the right of denunciation provided for in this Article, will be bound for another period of ten years and, thereafter, may denounce this Convention at the expiration of each period of ten years under the terms provided for in this Article.

Article 13

1. The Director-General of the International Labour Office shall notify all Members of the International Labour Organisation of the registration of all ratifications and denunciations communicated to him by the Members of the Organisation.

2. When notifying the Members of the Organisation of the registration of the second ratification communicated to him, the Director-General shall draw the attention of the Members of the Organisation to the date upon which the Convention will come into force.

Article 14

The Director-General of the International Labour Office shall communicate to the Secretary-General of the United Nations for registration in accordance with Article 102 of the Charter of the United Nations full particulars of all ratifications and acts of denunciation registered by him in accordance with the provisions of the preceding Articles.

Article 15

At such times as it may consider necessary the Governing Body of the International Labour Office shall present to the General Conference a report on the working of this Convention and shall examine the desirability of placing on the agenda of the Conference the question of its revision in whole or in part.

Article 16

1. Should the Conference adopt a new Convention revising this Convention in whole or in part, then, unless the new Convention otherwise provides—

(a) the ratification by a Member of the new revising Convention shall *ipso jure* involve the immediate denunciation of this Convention, notwithstanding the provisions of Article 12 above, if and when the new revising Convention shall have come into force;

(b) as from the date when the new revising Convention comes into force this Convention shall cease to be open to ratification by the Members.

2. This Convention shall in any case remain in force in its actual form and content for those Members which have ratified it but have not ratified the revising Convention.

Article 17

The English and French versions of the text of this Convention are equally authoritative.

RECOMMENDATION (No. 91) CONCERNING COLLECTIVE AGREEMENTS

The General Conference of the International Labour Organisation,

Having been convened at Geneva by the Governing Body of the International Labour Office, and having met in its Thirty-fourth Session on 6 June 1951, and

Having decided upon the adoption of certain proposals with regard to collective agreements, which is included in the fifth item on the agenda of the session, and

Having determined that these proposals shall take the form of a Recommendation designed to be implemented by the parties concerned or by the public authorities as may be appropriate under national conditions,

adopts this twenty-ninth day of June of the year one thousand nine hundred and fifty-one the following Recommendation, which may be cited as the Collective Agreements Recommendation, 1951 :

I. COLLECTIVE BARGAINING MACHINERY

1. (1) Machinery appropriate to the conditions existing in each country should be established, by means of agreement or laws or regulations as may be appropriate under national conditions, to negotiate, conclude, revise and renew collective agreements, or to be available to assist the parties in the negotiation, conclusion, revision and renewal of collective agreements.

(2) The organisation, methods of operation and functions of such machinery should be determined by agreements between the parties or by national laws or regulations, as may be appropriate under national conditions.

II. DEFINITION OF COLLECTIVE AGREEMENTS

2. (1) For the purpose of this Recommendation, the term " collective agreements " means all agreements in writing regarding working conditions and terms of employment concluded between an employer, a group of employers or one or more employers' organisations, on the one hand, and one or more representative workers' organisations, or, in the absence of such organisations, the representatives of the workers duly

elected and authorised by them in accordance with national laws and regulations, on the other.

(2) Nothing in the present definition should be interpreted as implying the recognition of any association of workers established, dominated or financed by employers or their representatives.

III. EFFECTS OF COLLECTIVE AGREEMENTS

3. (1) Collective agreements should bind the signatories thereto and those on whose behalf the agreement is concluded. Employers and workers bound by a collective agreement should not be able to include in contracts of employment stipulations contrary to those contained in the collective agreement.

(2) Stipulations in such contracts of employment which are contrary to a collective agreement should be regarded as null and void and automatically replaced by the corresponding stipulations of the collective agreement.

(3) Stipulations in contracts of employment which are more favourable to the workers than those prescribed by a collective agreement should not be regarded as contrary to the collective agreement.

(4) If effective observance of the provisions of collective agreements is secured by the parties thereto, the provisions of the preceding subparagraphs should not be regarded as calling for legislative measures.

4. The stipulations of a collective agreement should apply to all workers of the classes concerned employed in the undertakings covered by the agreement unless the agreement specifically provides to the contrary.

IV. EXTENSION OF COLLECTIVE AGREEMENTS

5. (1) Where appropriate, having regard to established collective bargaining practice, measures, to be determined by national laws or regulations and suited to the conditions of each country, should be taken to extend the application of all or certain stipulations of a collective agreement to all the employers and workers included within the industrial and territorial scope of the agreement.

(2) National laws or regulations may make the extension of a collective agreement subject to the following, among other, conditions :

(a) that the collective agreement already covers a number of the employers and workers concerned which is, in the opinion of the competent authority, sufficiently representative ;

(b) that, as a general rule, the request for extension of the agreement shall be made by one or more organisations of workers or employers who are parties to the agreement ;

(c) that, prior to the extension of the agreement, the employers and workers to whom the agreement would be made applicable by its extension should be given an opportunity to submit their observations.

V. INTERPRETATION OF COLLECTIVE AGREEMENTS

6. Disputes arising out of the interpretation of a collective agreement should be submitted to an appropriate procedure for settlement established either by agreement between the parties or by laws or regulations as may be appropriate under national conditions.

VI. SUPERVISION OF APPLICATION OF COLLECTIVE AGREEMENTS

7. The supervision of the application of collective agreements should be ensured by the employers' and workers' organisations parties to such agreements or by the bodies existing in each country for this purpose or by bodies established *ad hoc.*

VII. MISCELLANEOUS

8. National laws and regulations may, among other things, make provision for—

(a) requiring employers bound by collective agreements to take appropriate steps to bring to the notice of the workers concerned the texts of the collective agreements applicable to their undertakings ;

(b) the registration or deposit of collective agreements and any subsequent changes made therein ;

(c) a minimum period during which, in the absence of any provision to the contrary in the agreement, collective agreements shall be deemed to be binding unless revised or rescinded at an earlier date by the parties.

RECOMMENDATION CONCERNING
VOLUNTARY CONCILIATION AND ARBITRATION

The General Conference of the International Labour Organisation,

Having been convened at Geneva by the Governing Body of the International Labour Office, and having met in its Thirty-fourth Session on 6 June 1951, and

Having decided upon the adoption of certain proposals with regard to voluntary conciliation and arbitration, which is included in the fifth item on the agenda of the session, and

Having determined that these proposals shall take the form of a Recommendation designed to be implemented by the parties concerned or by the public authorities as may be appropriate under national conditions,

adopts this twenty-ninth day of June of the year one thousand nine hundred and fifty-one the following Recommendation, which may be cited as the Voluntary Conciliation and Arbitration Recommendation, 1951.

I. VOLUNTARY CONCILIATION

1. Voluntary conciliation machinery, appropriate to national conditions, should be made available to assist in the prevention and settlement of industrial disputes between employers and workers.

2. Where voluntary conciliation machinery is constituted on a joint basis, it should include equal representation of employers and workers.

3. (1) The procedure should be free of charge and expeditious ; such time limits for the proceedings as may be prescribed by national laws or regulations should be fixed in advance and kept to a minimum.

(2) Provision should be made to enable the procedure to be set in motion, either on the initiative of any of the parties to the dispute or ex officio by the voluntary conciliation authority.

4. If a dispute has been submitted to conciliation procedure with the consent of all the parties concerned, the latter should be encouraged to abstain from strikes and lockouts while conciliation is in progress.

5. All agreements which the parties may reach during conciliation procedure or as a result thereof should be drawn up in writing and be regarded as equivalent to agreements concluded in the usual manner.

II. Voluntary Arbitration

6.   If a dispute has been submitted to arbitration for final settlement with the consent of all parties concerned, the latter should be encouraged to abstain from strikes and lockouts while the arbitration is in progress and to accept the arbitration award.

III. General

7.   No provision of this Recommendation may be interpreted as limiting, in any way whatsoever, the right to strike.

Recommendation 158

RECOMMENDATION CONCERNING LABOUR ADMINISTRATION: ROLE, FUNCTIONS AND ORGANISATION

The General Conference of the International Labour Organisation,

Having been convened at Geneva by the Governing Body of the International Labour Office, and having met in its Sixty-fourth Session on 7 June 1978, and

Recalling the terms of existing international labour Conventions and Recommendations, including in particular the Labour Inspection Convention, 1947, the Labour Inspection (Agriculture) Convention, 1969, and the Employment Service Convention, 1948, which call for the exercise of particular labour administration activities, and

Considering it desirable to adopt instruments establishing guidelines regarding the over-all system of labour administration, and

Recalling the terms of the Employment Policy Convention, 1964, and of the Human Resources Development Convention, 1975; recalling also the goal of the creation of full and adequately remunerated employment and affirming the need for programmes of labour administration to work towards this goal and to give effect to the objectives of the said Conventions, and

Recognising the necessity of fully respecting the autonomy of employers' and workers' organisations, recalling in this connection the terms of existing international labour Conventions and Recommendations guaranteeing rights of association, organisation and collective bargaining—and particularly the Freedom of Association and Protection of the Right to Organise Convention, 1948, and the Right to Organise and Collective Bargaining Convention, 1949—which forbid any interference by public authorities which would restrict these rights or impede the lawful exercise thereof, and considering that employers' and workers' organisations have essential roles in attaining the objectives of economic, social and cultural progress, and

Having decided upon the adoption of certain proposals with regard to labour administration: role, functions and organisation, which is the fourth item on the agenda of the session, and

Having determined that these proposals shall take the form of a Recommendation supplementing the Labour Administration Convention, 1978,

adopts this twenty-sixth day of June of the year one thousand nine hundred and seventy-eight the following Recommendation, which may be cited as the Labour Administration Recommendation, 1978:

I. GENERAL PROVISIONS

1. For the purpose of this Recommendation—

(a) the term " labour administration " means public administration activities in the field of national labour policy;

(b) the term " system of labour administration " covers all public administration bodies responsible for and/or engaged in labour administration—whether they are ministerial departments or public agencies, including parastatal and regional or local agencies or any other form of decentralised administration—and any institutional framework for the co-ordination of the activities of such bodies and for consultation with and participation by employers and workers and their organisations.

2. A Member may, in accordance with national laws or regulations, or national practice, delegate or entrust certain activities of labour administration to non-governmental organisations, particularly employers' and workers' organisations, or—where appropriate—to employers' and workers' representatives.

3. A Member may regard particular activities in the field of its national labour policy as being matters which, in accordance with national laws or regulations, or national practice, are regulated by having recourse to direct negotiations between employers' and workers' organisations.

4. Each Member should, in a manner appropriate to national conditions, ensure the organisation and effective operation in its territory of a system of labour administration, the functions and responsibilities of which are properly co-ordinated.

II. FUNCTIONS OF THE NATIONAL SYSTEM OF LABOUR ADMINISTRATION

Labour Standards

5. (1) The competent bodies within the system of labour administration should—in consultation with organisations of employers and workers and in a manner and under conditions determined by national laws or regulations, or national practice—take an active part in the preparation, development, adoption, application and review of labour standards, including relevant laws and regulations.

(2) They should make their services available to employers' and workers' organisations, as may be appropriate under national laws or regulations, or national practice, with a view to promoting the regulation of terms and conditions of employment by means of collective bargaining.

6. The system of labour administration should include a system of labour inspection.

Labour Relations

7. The competent bodies within the system of labour administration should participate in the determination and application of such measures as may be necessary to ensure the free exercise of employers' and workers' right of association.

8. (1) There should be labour administration programmes aimed at the promotion, establishment and pursuit of labour relations which encourage progressively better conditions of work and working life and which respect the right to organise and bargain collectively.

(2) The competent bodies within the system of labour administration should assist in the improvement of labour relations by providing or strengthening advisory services to undertakings, employers' organisations and workers' organisations requesting such services, in accordance with programmes established on the basis of consultation with such organisations.

9. The competent bodies within the system of labour administration should promote the full development and utilisation of machinery for voluntary negotiation.

10. The competent bodies within the system of labour administration should be in a position to provide, in agreement with the employers' and workers' organisations concerned, conciliation and mediation facilities, appropriate to national conditions, in case of collective disputes.

Employment

11. (1) The competent bodies within the system of labour administration should be responsible for or participate in the preparation, administration, co-ordination, checking and review of national employment policy.

(2) A central body of the system of labour administration, to be determined in accordance with national laws or regulations, or national practice, should be closely associated with, or responsible for taking, appropriate institutional measures to co-ordinate the activities of the various authorities and bodies which are concerned with particular aspects of employment policy.

12. The competent bodies within the system of labour administration should co-ordinate, or participate in the co-ordination of, employment services, employment promotion and creation programmes, vocational guidance and vocational training programmes and unemployment benefit schemes, and they should co-ordinate, or participate in the co-ordination of, these various services, programmes and schemes with the implementation of general employment policy measures.

13. The competent bodies within the system of labour administration should be responsible for establishing, or promoting the establishment of, methods and procedures for ensuring consultation of employers' and workers' organisations, or—where appropriate—employers' and workers' representatives, on employment policies, and promotion of their co-operation in the implementation of such policies.

14. (1) The competent bodies within the system of labour administration should be responsible for manpower planning or where this is not possible should participate in the functioning of manpower planning bodies through both institutional representation and the provision of technical information and advice.

(2) They should participate in the co-ordination and integration of manpower plans with economic plans.

(3) They should promote joint action of employers and workers, with the assistance as appropriate of public authorities and bodies, regarding both short- and long-term employment policies.

15. The system of labour administration should include a free public employment service and operate such a service effectively.

16. The competent bodies within the system of labour administration should, wherever national laws and regulations, or national practice, so permit, have or share responsibility for the management of public funds made available for such purposes as countering underemployment and unemployment, regulating the regional distribution of employment, or promoting and assisting the employment of particular categories of workers, including sheltered employment schemes.

17. The competent bodies within the system of labour administration should, in a manner and under conditions determined by national laws or regulations, or

national practice, participate in the development of comprehensive and concerted policies and programmes of human resources development including vocational guidance and vocational training.

Research in Labour Matters

18. For the fulfilment of its social objectives, the system of labour administration should carry out research as one of its important functions and encourage research by others.

III. ORGANISATION OF THE NATIONAL SYSTEM OF LABOUR ADMINISTRATION

Co-ordination

19. The ministry of labour or another comparable body determined by national laws or regulations, or national practice, should take or initiate measures ensuring appropriate representation of the system of labour administration in the administrative and consultative bodies in which information is collected, opinions are considered, decisions are prepared and taken and measures of implementation are devised with respect to social and economic policies.

20. (1) Each of the principal labour administration services competent with respect to the matters referred to in Paragraphs 5 to 18 above should provide periodic information or reports on its activities to the ministry of labour or the other comparable body referred to in Paragraph 19, as well as to employers' and workers' organisations.

(2) Such information or reports should be of a technical nature, include appropriate statistics, and indicate the problems encountered and if possible the results achieved in such a manner as to permit an evaluation of present trends and foreseeable future developments in areas of major concern to the system of labour administration.

(3) The system of labour administration should evaluate, publish and disseminate such information of general interest on labour matters as it is able to derive from its operation.

(4) Members, in consultation with the International Labour Office, should seek to promote the establishment of suitable models for the publication of such information, with a view to improving its international comparability.

21. The structures of the national system of labour administration should be kept constantly under review, in consultation with the most representative organisations of employers and workers.

Resources and Staff

22. (1) Appropriate arrangements should be made to provide the system of labour administration with the necessary financial resources and an adequate number of suitably qualified staff to promote its effectiveness.

(2) In this connection, due account should be taken of—

(a) the importance of the duties to be performed;

(b) the material means placed at the disposal of the staff;

(c) the practical conditions under which the various functions must be carried out in order to be effective.

23. (1) The staff of the labour administration system should receive initial and further training at levels suitable for their work; there should be permanent arrangements to ensure that such training is available to them throughout their careers.

(2) Staff in particular services should have the special qualifications required for such services, ascertained in a manner determined by the appropriate body.

24. Consideration should be given to supplementing national programmes and facilities for the training envisaged in Paragraph 23 above by international co-operation in the form of exchanges of experience and information and of common initial and further training programmes and facilities, particularly at the regional level.

Internal Organisation

25. (1) The system of labour administration should normally comprise specialised units to deal with each of the major programmes of labour administration the management of which is entrusted to it by national laws or regulations.

(2) For example, there might be units for such matters as the formulation of standards relating to working conditions and terms of employment; labour inspection; labour relations; employment, manpower planning and human resources development; international labour affairs; and, as appropriate, social security, minimum wage legislation and questions relating to specific categories of workers.

Field Services

26. (1) There should be appropriate arrangements for the effective organisation and operation of the field services of the system of labour administration.

(2) In particular, these arrangements should—

(a) ensure that the placing of field services corresponds to the needs of the various areas, the representative organisations of employers and workers concerned being consulted thereon;

(b) provide field services with adequate staff, equipment and transport facilities for the effective performance of their duties;

(c) ensure that field services have sufficient and clear instructions to preclude the possibility of laws and regulations being differently interpreted in different areas.

Recommendation 159

RECOMMENDATION CONCERNING PROCEDURES FOR DETERMINING CONDITIONS OF EMPLOYMENT IN THE PUBLIC SERVICE

The General Conference of the International Labour Organisation,

Having been convened at Geneva by the Governing Body of the International Labour Office, and having met in its Sixty-fourth Session on 7 June 1978, and

Having decided upon the adoption of certain proposals with regard to freedom of association and procedures for determining conditions of employment in the public service, which is the fifth item on the agenda of the session, and

Having determined that these proposals shall take the form of a Recommendation supplementing the Labour Relations (Public Service) Convention, 1978,

adopts this twenty-seventh day of June of the year one thousand nine hundred and seventy-eight the following Recommendation, which may be cited as the Labour Relations (Public Service) Recommendation, 1978:

1. (1) In countries in which procedures for recognition of public employees' organisations apply with a view to determining the organisations to be granted, on a preferential or exclusive basis, the rights provided for under Parts III, IV or V of the Labour Relations (Public Service) Convention, 1978, such determination should be based on objective and pre-established criteria with regard to the organisations' representative character.

(2) The procedures referred to in subparagraph (1) of this Paragraph should be such as not to encourage the proliferation of organisations covering the same categories of employees.

2. (1) In the case of negotiation of terms and conditions of employment in accordance with Part IV of the Labour Relations (Public Service) Convention, 1978, the persons or bodies competent to negotiate on behalf of the public authority concerned and the procedure for giving effect to the agreed terms and conditions of employment should be determined by national laws or regulations or other appropriate means.

(2) Where methods other than negotiation are followed to allow representatives of public employees to participate in the determination of terms and conditions of employment, the procedure for such participation and for final determination of these matters should be determined by national laws or regulations or other appropriate means.

3. Where an agreement is concluded between a public authority and a public employees' organisation in pursuance of Paragraph 2, subparagraph (1), of this Recommendation, the period during which it is to operate and/or the procedure whereby it may be terminated, renewed or revised should normally be specified.

4. In determining the nature and scope of the facilities which should be afforded to representatives of public employees' organisations in accordance with Article 6, paragraph 3, of the Labour Relations (Public Service) Convention, 1978, regard should be had to the Workers' Representatives Recommendation, 1971.

ANNEX 4

Some other useful ILO publications.

Workers' Education and Its Techniques (ISBN 92-2-100195-4)

This manual has been developed to provide in a simple and easily handled form a survey of the main problems and modern practices of workers' education. On the basis of a discussion of the ends of workers' education it outlines some of the means by which these objectives may be accomplished.

Collective Bargaining (ISBN 92-2-100078-8)

This workers' education manual consists of 12 lessons dealing successively with the definition and origins of collective bargaining, the conditions essential to its success, how it works, the subject matters of collective bargaining and agreements, the practical application of agreements, procedures for settlement of disputes, unfair labour practices, various consequences of breakdown in collective bargaining, conciliation and arbitration, and the attitude of national authorities towards collective bargaining. The manual may be used by the instructor running courses in collective bargaining or by the students themselves.

How to Read a Balance Sheet (ISBN 92-2-100000-1)

A useful aid for anyone who needs to be able to understand and analyse a company's financial position and operations, e.g. a collective bargainer, a union representative on a company board.

Conciliation in Industrial Disputes (ISBN 92-2-101007-4)
Grievance Arbitration (ISBN 92-2-101722-2)

Both the above guides have been published with a view to providing practical guidance for persons serving as conciliators or arbitrators on how to establish procedures and carry out the tasks. They will, at the same time, be equally useful for trade union and employers' representatives charged with the task of representing their members to understand the process and to make the best possible impact.

Trade Unions and the ILO (ISBN 92-2-102003-7)

This workers' education manual has been published with a view to supplementing earlier workers' education publications by suggesting ways in which trade unionists can learn how the ILO works, the ways in which trade unions participate in its conferences and contribute to the development and improvement of international labour standards for the purpose of improving industrial relations and minimum working standards throughout the world.

Note: Information concerning prices and the placing of orders for any publication may be done under the following address: International Laboaur Office, Publications, CH-1211 Geneva 22, Switzerland.